PLAYING CARDS

Series editor: Frédérique Crestin-Billet
Translated from the French by Roland Glasser
Copy-editing and typesetting by Kate van den Boogert
Design by Lélie Carnot
Color separation by Chesteroc Graphics
Originally published as La Folie des Cartes à Jouer
© 2002 Flammarion, Paris
English-language edition © 2002 Flammarion, Inc.

ISBN: 2-0801-1134-5
Printed in France

Collectible
PLAYING CARDS

Frédérique Crestin-Billet

Flammarion

When I was a child my grandmother and I would indulge in fierce rummy sessions during the long evenings of the summer vacation. I loved those cards so much that I could have drawn virtually every detail of them from memory—kings, queens, jacks and all. One rainy day thirty years later, while scouring a secondhand shop for some playing cards to amuse my daughters with, I was surprised to come across an old Italian deck of cards whose suit symbols and court cards were completely different from those I was familiar with. I decided to find out more...

CONTENTS

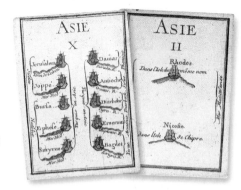

Introduction

Although everyone knows what playing cards are, their precise origin remains a mystery. For decades specialists have argued all sorts of contradictory theories. Some believe they were brought to Europe from India by gypsies; others argue that they were invented to entertain the Chinese emperor Houei-Tsong's concubines in the year 1120. But Egypt, Italy, Germany and Spain also claim paternity...

There are even authors who—perhaps to make up for an unnerving lack of specific information—have supported an array of claims as to the origin of playing cards that are far too precise to be plausible. In the eighteenth century it was claimed that playing cards were invented in 1392 to entertain King Charles IV of France during one of his spells of dementia. A little later a certain Abbot Rive, a partisan of Spanish origin, wrote that they had "been invented by one Nicolas Pépin. The Spanish word for them, *naipes*, comes from the letters N.P., which are the initials of their inventor."

But although their origin remains obscure, the dates when they appeared in Europe are clearer. In his book on the subject, Roger Tilley affirms that "fixing a date is made easier by the following negative proof:

> 1365—playing cards are not mentioned in the instructions given to clerics by the abbot of Saint Germain, who forbade certain games of dice or chance on pain of being deprived of wine for a week(!).
>
> 1369—playing cards are not mentioned in a decree given by Charles V against gambling.
>
> 1375—no allusion to playing cards is made either by Petrarch (1304–74) or by his friend Boccaccio (1313–75), although they cite other amusements and games."

Detail of a poster from the House of Grimaud. This figure was drawn at the end of the nineteenth century and became the emblem of the card manufacturer who, between 1850 and 1900, had acquired a virtual monopoly on the production of playing cards in France.

However, in 1379 cards were banned in the German town of Ratisbonne, and a year later an accounting ledger of the Duchy of Brabant mentions a payment for the purchase of *speelquarten*, or playing cards. In 1381 an undertaking made in the presence of a Marseille solicitor by Jacques Jean, son of a merchant in the town and soon to be embarking for Alexandria, stipulates that he will refrain from practicing any games of chance, including cards. A few years later the provost of Paris prohibited the playing of cards, tennis, boules, dice and skittles on working days. It is clear that by the end of the fourteenth century, playing cards had appeared in Europe.

Lithographic reproduction of a Dutch painting—the card game would appear to be hotly disputed. From the very start the authorities attempted to ban card games because of the endless hours people spent playing instead of working! As for the Church, its opposition was just as fierce, seeing in card games the hand of the devil.

Valet of Clubs (battoni) from an Italian deck made by Viassone in 1970.

Questions concerning the choice of suit symbols are just as obscure and fascinating as those concerning the origins of the cards. The oldest decks found in Europe always show four suits. The first pips used came from the Tarot—clubs, coins, cups and swords. These are now termed Latin pips and are still used in Italy and Spain.

Other pips then appeared. The first known German cards display a series of pips, illustrated with various animals. These symbols remained in use until the second half of the fifteenth century, when they were replaced by the current German pips— hearts, bells, leaves and acorns.

But did France, with her pikes, hearts, tiles and clovers, follow or precede Germany in the choice of a set of pips that was different from the Latin one? The question remains unanswered.

A signed deck by François Clerc, who worked in Lyon between 1485 and 1486, shows crescents instead of tiles. Was this just an imaginative exception, or were French pips only defined after 1490? This question, too, remains unanswered. Moreover, it is interesting to note that although the French pips were exported to England, the translation of their names

Six of Leaves
(laube or grüne) from a recent Bavarian deck.

does not indicate their country of origin: the pike was called a spade (from the Italian *spada*, or sword), the clover became the club—these two names are clearly influenced by the Latin pips— while the tile was called a diamond, where the term lozenge would perhaps have been more appropriate. Only the heart was translated literally from the French. Many suppositions have been made concerning the significance of these pips; but again, all we have are hypotheses, whatever the country.

Some have seen the various classes of society represented by these suit symbols: swords, cups, coins and clubs would represent respectively the aristocracy, the Church, merchants and peasants. Others have seen virtues or vices in them. The sword would symbolize justice or war, the club courage or violence, the coin charity or greed, and the cup

A rare deck of miniature cards with German pips from the eighteenth century:
hearts (herzen), leaves (grün or laub) and, above, acorns (eicheln).
The bells (schellen) are not pictured here.

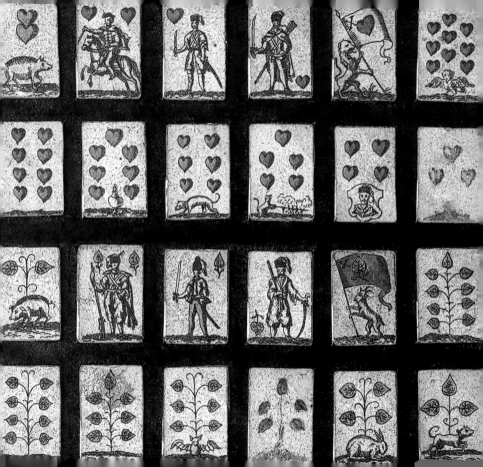

faith or drunkenness. The same loose reasoning has been applied to the French pips—the heart is for the clergy, the pikes for officers of the military nobility, tiles for the houses of the bourgeoisie, and the clover represents the countryside, or peasantry.

In 1720 one P. Daniel suggested that a game of cards was like a game of war, with the clover for the horses' fodder, the heart for the courage of the combatants, the pike for the arms, and the tile for the heavy bolts fired by crossbows. This may seem a little far-fetched, but the German suit symbols are no more eloquent, even if people have claimed to see the nobility represented by the bells, the Church by the hearts, the citizenry by the leaves, and the peasantry by the acorns.

At a time when cardboard was still rare, cards were used for a variety of purposes other than that for which they were made, as can be seen from these examples dating from the eighteenth century. Uses included shopping lists and reinforcement for book bindings. Lace and embroidery workers bought rejects at a heavy discount. The large printed sheets, from which the cards would have been cut were it not for printing or design errors, served as useful mounts for them to pin their stencils to.

But one thing is certain—playing cards soon became very popular, so the pips had to be familiar to populations that were mostly illiterate. The wisest thing might well be to draw parallels with heraldic imagery, since there appears to be a clear, though unexplained, link between the two.

The figures depicted on the cards were usually anonymous, at least up until the end of the sixteenth century, and might represent a very wide range of characters. There was a trend, still followed in Italy today, of "portraits," or characteristic ways of representing people according to the region they came from. French card-makers, whose production was starting to outstrip that of Germany, had the idea of giving these figures names taken from the Bible, antiquity, medieval epic poems, history and even contemporary life; examples include King David, Judith, Alexander the Great and Joan of Arc. It was only in the middle of the seventeenth century that these names were standardized, although this process was interrupted by the French

This anonymous King of Clubs from Auvergne is reprinted from a deck that appeared originally in 1640. You can see other cards from this deck on pages 42 and 43.

Revolution (see page 58).

It is generally thought that the kings represent the four traditional kingdoms, although these assumptions have their own detractors. But according to this concept, spades are represented by King David of the Israelites, clubs by King Alexander of the Greeks, hearts by King Charlemagne of the Franks, and diamonds by the Roman emperor Julius Caesar. As for the queens, they are not the true consorts of these

The King of Diamonds on the left comes from a Dutch deck, that on the right from Liège. These are narrow miner's cards from the end of the nineteenth century. Notice that they are without corner indices, which denote the values of the cards. Such indices have been added to the reprint of the King of Clubs on the facing page, since the original cards did not include them.

sovereigns but represent the four virtues by which women may reign. Diamonds are graced by Rachel (beauty), hearts by Judith (piety), spades by Pallas (wisdom), and clubs by Argine (anagram of regina, the Latin word for queen, and representing birth).

As for the jacks, hearts are served by La Hire (a courageous captain and loyal companion of Joan of Arc in the battle against the English), spades by Ogier (a legendary hero who married Morgan Le Fay, King Arthur's sorceress sister), clubs by Lancelot (one of the most celebrated knights of the Round Table) and diamonds by Hector, although there is much conjecture as to whether this is the Sir Hector who fostered the future King Arthur, or Hector de Galard, who served King Charles V. Whatever the truth of the matter, this collection of characters is as strange as it is amusing and very much in the French, even Parisian, tradition, since all the various regional face-designs of the jack were eventually replaced by that of Paris, the youngest son of King Priam and cause of the fall of Troy.

Serious card players are conservative in their attitude towards card illustration. One's concentration may easily be disturbed by a deck of cards bearing unfamiliar decorations or face-designs. This explains why kings, queens and jacks are stuck in their somewhat curious fifteenth-century costumes and poses!

As you read these pages you will discover some of the incredible diversity that playing cards have to offer. As with all of the books in this *Collectibles* series, the aim is a simple one—to reveal a world whose richness you had perhaps not suspected. And it is indeed an abundant world, for apart from the millions of traditional decks of cards printed each year by today's card-makers, there are also a great many reprints of the beautiful decks of yesterday, as well as some lovely new designs. Having read these pages you will never look at a playing card in quite the same way again.

Many brands have used the imagery of playing cards to sell their products, as in this magnificent poster by the artist Job advertising luxury cars.

Affiches RENÉ CARÊME, 110 Avenue d'Orléans, PARIS

I

GAME

playing cards

Everyone is familiar with the deck of cards traditionally used in their own country, with the modern English model clearly the most well known overall. But every country has its own traditions when it comes to playing cards, and various regions of a particular country also add their own touches. This chapter invites you to discover cards with origins in countries as diverse as France, Switzerland, Belgium, Germany, Russia, Sweden, Hungary, Italy and Spain. Those of you who thought that your family playing cards would yield no more secrets, prepare to be surprised, and surrender yourselves to this fabulous voyage, for these cards constitute a marvelous odyssey through space and time.

These days, particularly in the English-speaking world, we are used to a single type of card. But it has not always been like this; for example, sixteenth-century France saw a gradual definition of various regional face-designs or patterns.

As was mentioned in the introduction (see page 14), the authorities, in particular the Church, did not always approve of playing cards. But faced with a growing enthusiasm for them, the state quickly realized that there was a profit to be made by levying a duty on them. With card-makers fiercely opposing this, the seventeenth century saw alternating periods of imposition of and freedom from such a tax.

The trend towards fixed symbols in France began in 1701 when a limited number of card-makers in just a few authorized towns were obliged to conform to the conventions of their region as regards card illustration. Nine regional patterns were chosen by the authorities, including those of Lyon. Their principal characteristics were this jack smoking a pipe and kings brandishing scepters topped with the fleur-de-lis. This card, as well as those on the two preceding pages, is part of a Lyon deck that dates from after 1751 and was printed by Fayolle.

Lyon was a major French card-making center in the fifteenth century and so had considerable influence on the card patterns of the surrounding regions. The Burgundy pattern—of which this king from an eighteenth-century deck is an example—was copied from the Lyon pattern. But it stands out due to its more geometric design and the kings' crowns, which are exceptionally wide. One of nine official patterns, the Burgundy deck was printed chiefly in Dijon, although there exist editions from Besançon and Lyon.

The pattern from the Dauphiné region in southeast France was also based on the Lyon pattern. The kings and queens both hold scepters with fleur-de-lis, but the jack has some rather strange characteristics. As you can see on this card dating from between the end of the seventeenth century and the beginning of the eighteenth, this Jack of Diamonds is accompanied by an enigmatic inscription that we also find in Burgundy, and the knees of his britches are decorated with human heads.

As for the Jack of Hearts, he proclaims "Shush!" while raising his forefinger; and the Jacks of Clubs and Spades are dressed in the style of the sixteenth century. In addition, the latter bears the name of the card-maker, Bermond. The card on the facing page is the work of another card-maker, Claude Bouvard. Both were probably based in Grenoble which, along with another French town, Romans, was the principal location for production of the Dauphiné pattern.

Produced in all the major towns in the south of France—Marseille, Avignon, Aix, Toulon, Nîmes and Montpellier—the Provençal pattern is also derived from the Lyon model. The card shown here is a Queen of Diamonds. Note that the diamond is uncharacteristically black in color; the accompanying text reads, Vive les bons enfans qui jouent souvent, or "Long live all good children who play a lot."

One of the many characteristics of the Provençal pattern is that the Jack of Hearts is shown face-on, with his right hand placed jauntily on his hip and his left holding a halberd. The name of the card-maker seems so contrived that one might easily mistake it for a crafty marketing ploy of the twenty-first century! But no, a certain Esprit Trescartes, or "Spirit Verycards," really did live and work in Carpentras from 1735 to 1742.

Although the Provençal queens are quite similar to those from Lyon, this Queen of Hearts from the eighteenth century has the particularity of being bare breasted, as well as having her limbs covered in scales. This was perhaps due to the proximity of the Mediterranean Sea, hinting at mermaids or other superstitions, while the sun on her cloak and flower in her hand clearly evoke the south.

Another card from the Provençal pattern and taken from a deck printed by Jean Payen, a family card-making firm in Avignon. Tradition is well respected here, with the Jack of Spades wearing his hair plaited, a particularity that we also find on the Jack of Clubs, as well as on various jacks from other regional patterns.

The Auvergne pattern
may be considered a
dominant one, just like
those of Lyon and Paris
(mentioned later on),
since it inspired the
patterns from the
Limoges, Guyenne and
Languedoc regions.
These two kings come
from an eighteenth-
century deck.

How many people know that the town of Thiers, in the Auvergne region of France, which would achieve world celebrity in the nineteenth century for its cutlery, was once a highly reputed center of card making, flooding many countries, including Spain, with its packs of cards? The decline of Thiers's card-making industry, whose prosperity dated from the fifteenth century, started with the Spanish war, followed by the levying of taxes in 1701 (see page 31), then by the establishment of a royal card-printing works at Clermont-Ferrand in 1748.

Jehan Volay was
one of the most
celebrated card-
makers of Thiers.
These two modern
cards are reprints
made by Dusserre
of a deck Volay
produced around
1640. The originals
are stored in the
French National
Library.

Apart from the orb held by the King of Hearts (see page 41), the principal characteristics of the Auvergne pattern are the breastplates and helmets of the jacks. The Queen of Spades cradles a little dog, while the King of Hearts sometimes has a parrot, but only sometimes, since both dog and parrot were excluded from all decks intended for export.

There exist versions of the
Auvergne pattern where
the Jack of Spades, wearing
helmet and breastplate
according to tradition, bears
the lion of Thiers on his
chest. The lion is not present
on this eighteenth-century
card by Perol. This is
doubtless due to the creeping
influence of the Paris pattern.
Originally the Auvergne deck
did not include the card-
maker's name.

The Guyenne pattern is inspired largely by the Auvergne pattern—of which the Limoges pattern is a rough copy. However, the King of Diamonds carries a scepter surmounted, curiously enough, by a heart and then an eye! The author of this eighteenth-century card is unknown. The Guyenne pattern was produced chiefly in Bordeaux and Agen.

Two queens from the Languedoc pattern, another regional model and largely inspired by that of Auvergne. However, the deck does have one particularity—the King of Diamonds holds a purse in his hand, while the scepter he carries is surmounted by a crescent. These cards were manufactured largely in Toulouse, but the model was also used in Carcassonne, Albi and Béziers. As for these two

queens of unknown author,
they hail from Montauban. All
of these older decks were
printed using the technique
of wood engraving and were
then colored using stencils.
The historian and expert on
cards and games Thierry
Depaulis has devoted
considerable study to these
cards. Most of the information
in these pages has been
gleaned from the various
books he has written
(see page 376).

When a levy on playing cards was imposed in France in 1701, resulting in an inevitable reorganization of their production (see page 31), certain patterns disappeared completely, notably that of Rouen. It was decided that in view of the relative proximity of the town to Paris, it should come under its wing, at least as far as playing cards were concerned. But this change of affairs was not a total loss. For when the Edict of Nantes (signed by Henry IV of France in 1598 and guaranteeing relative tolerance for Protestants in France) was revoked in 1685, the Protestant card-makers of Rouen emigrated to England.

... England was probably chosen by the Rouen card-makers for the strong commercial links that had long existed between it and the Normandy region. The Rouen pattern thus gave birth to the English pattern, as can be seen from a comparison of these two cards. On the left is an eighteenth-century card taken from a deck printed by Adolphe Thomas (card-maker to the royal family). The card on the right is taken from a modern deck. Of course, a whole series of modernizations and personal touches from various card-makers were involved in determining the deck of cards with which we are familiar today.

The Paris pattern goes back to the sixteenth century and is the source for contemporary French cards. Its principal characteristic is the attribution of names to the various characters. Although no precise information exists concerning the decisions that lay behind the choice of these names, you will find further information on this matter on pages 22 to 24.

The Paris pattern has undergone a series of modifications over time, just like the English pattern mentioned on the preceding pages. Taken from a deck produced by the card-maker François-Henri Cadine, these two cards are considered to be of the 1778 type, meaning that they predate the temporary disappearance of the Paris pattern during the Revolution. Notice the necklace worn by the Queen of Spades, which has disappeared from the current version of the card.

Despite its name, the Paris pattern was not restricted to the capital but was used throughout a large part of northern France, from Brittany to Normandy to Touraine to Picardy to the Artois region to Champagne, as shown by this Jack of Clubs from a deck signed by Pierre Pavie of Troyes. The Paris pattern was also imposed on Alsace and Lorraine from 1751, although the card-makers of Metz, Nancy, Strasbourg and Épinal did not respect the law and carried on producing cards with their local designs.

On older versions of this card Argine holds a flower in her hand, but in 1701 this was replaced by a fan. Argine would continue to hold her fan as long as figures on cards were depicted in full-length format, as seen here (also on page 65). But the fan disappeared with the introduction of the double-ended format that we know today.

The suit symbols that have become the most widespread across the world have their origin in French playing cards, and for some very sound economical and practical reasons. For since the pips on each card were a single color, they required but a single stamp to print them. The Germans, Swiss and Italians, however, were obliged to use wood engravings for their bells, coins and cups, with colorings that were often quite elaborate. It just goes to show that sometimes genius may be found in simplicity.

However, too much simplicity is not always a good thing either. Although the extreme sobriety of these pip cards may be aesthetically pleasing, the lack of corner indices is quite a handicap for today's player. The corner indices consist of letters or numbers that indicate either the figure or the number of pips that appear on the cards themselves.

*Tall and straight, these pip cards are from around
1880. Often produced using a very stiff cardboard, these
decks are also known as "miner's cards." The card on the
left-hand page and those on the two preceding pages are
taken from an eighteenth-century French deck.*

As it did in so many domains, the Revolution brought major changes to playing cards. The breath of apparent liberty that spread through all society at the beginning soon gave way to a range of strictures and regulations. Two of these had a considerable effect on the manufacture of playing cards. Guilds were abolished in 1791 and all signs of "royalty and feudality" forbidden.

Kings were thus converted into wise men; in this deck by Pinaut from 1794 they are personified by Rousseau, Solon, Cato and Brutus. As for the queens, they are replaced by the cardinal virtues—Justice, Prudence, Courage and Temperance— while the jacks become lusty young men.

Although some decks produced during the Revolution were the imaginative work of great Paris card-makers like Antoine Lefer, Jean Minot Sr. or even Chassonneris, others were simply reprints of existing models, like this anonymous Jack of Diamonds portraying Courage.

This Liberty of Spades' crown has been snatched off rather hastily, resulting in the back of her head being strangely flat!

A reprint of a deck of cards from the Revolution, designed by Saint-Simon and manufactured by the Parisian card-maker Jaume & Dugourc in 1793. Kings have been replaced by the Spirits of Commerce, the Arts, War and Peace (although this card sports Industry as its subject); queens were replaced by the Liberties of Marriage, the Press, the Professions and Religions.

... As for the jacks, they came to personify equalities—Rights, Duties, Peoples and Rank. Many decks like these were produced, deploying antique personnages as contemporary symbols. One deck produced in Toulouse in 1794 had kings of the elements, queens of the seasons and farmer jacks!

After the confusion of the Revolution, various attempts to find a unique design for the entire empire followed; it was the version produced by the engraver Nicolas-Marie Gatteaux that was finally selected in 1813.

What was once the Paris pattern now became the French pattern. The two cards on this page are old enough that their figures are still depicted in full-length format. Although the quality of the illustration has certainly gained in finesse, it has lost much of the undoubted charm of the seventeenth-century cards. Yet these are clearly the ancestors of our modern playing cards.

The official French pattern received its double-end around 1830, and apart from a few details, it has hardly changed since. The card shown here is based on a model from 1853 but was printed in the 1890s; of squatter size than some of its predecessors, it is a copperplate engraving colored with stencils. The name of the card-maker is unknown, but the paper on which the deck was printed is clearly watermarked, as was required by the law of the time concerning the taxation of gaming, including playing cards.

It was only in 1945 that the tax on gaming was reduced, before being definitively lifted a few years later. This liberalization of the industry enabled French card-makers to offer different models than the hitherto ubiquitous French pattern. This is a lovely example, although the name of the author remains unknown.

This card was commissioned in 1978 from the artist Henri Simoni by Dusserre. Whether due to the suddenness of the change or the conservatism of card players, this deck was not as successful as had been hoped.

This queen was produced in the 1950s and is a Franco-Swiss pattern—in other words, a Swiss variant of the French pattern. This deck was printed by Müller, of Schaffhouse, the card-maker who introduced the double-ended court card in 1908. Notice that the line bisects the figure horizontally, and not diagonally, as on the French pattern.

Caught between two cultures, Switzerland has always produced and used both French cards, or French-inspired cards (as demonstrated by the pattern on the preceding page), and German cards.

But Switzerland also developed its own suit symbols—the bell, the shield, the rose and the acorn—as can be seen from this nineteenth-century deck by Johann David Hurters.

KÖNIG

Typically, Swiss decks of playing cards, just like German ones, do not have queens. The queen is replaced by a "higher" jack called obermann, or ober, partnered by a "lower" jack called untermann, or unter (see preceding page). Ober actually corresponds to the knight in the Tarot deck. This Ober of Coins bears similarities to the pipe-smoking jacks of the Lyon and Dauphiné patterns (see page 32), regions close to Switzerland.

Another particularity of the Swiss decks is the deuce, or daus, that displaces the ace as the highest card. These are always decorated with banners or oriflammes, as we see on this reprint from a deck from 1830 by Johann David Hurters.

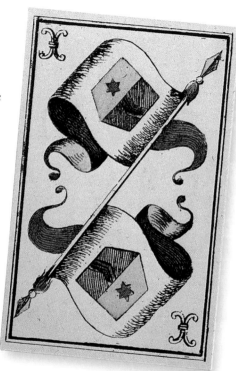

A nineteenth-century Swiss
deck with French suit
symbols. The full-length
pattern from Geneva is
inspired by the Paris deck.
For more than two centuries,
trends in Geneva have closely
followed those of Paris (see
also pages 226 and 227).

Another Swiss deck with
French suit symbols, doubtless
intended for nineteenth-century
tourists. Each ace is illustrated
with two landscapes. The figures
are drawn after the Paris pattern
in a romantic manner.

– 75 –

This King of Hearts and this
Jack of Clubs come from a
deck printed in the 1950s by
Müller. They are in the style
of the Neuchâtel pattern,
one of the decks with French
suit symbols traditionally
produced by Swiss card-
makers. It was introduced
to Switzerland at the end of
the eighteenth century by
French card-makers fleeing
an over-zealous fiscal policy!

The Neuchâtel pattern
is strongly inspired by
that of Lyon, although
certain figures lack the
finesse of the original.
Specificities of the deck
include the plaited hair
of this jack and a head-
dress with visor worn
by the Queen of Hearts.
Also, the aces are
decorated, as is the
case with many
Swiss decks.

A Queen of Spades after the
Liège pattern. An uncommon
deck, it was derived from
the Rouen pattern and
would appear to fit the trend
of narrow cards with figures
depicted in full-length
format that was in vogue in
Holland in the eighteenth
century. This miner's deck
(see page 57) comes from
a deck printed by Brepols
of Turnhout.

The Brussels pattern appeared around 1800 and is one of the many derived from the Paris pattern, the main difference being that the King of Spades has lost his harp. This card, also narrow, comes from a deck dating from 1890. The Brussels pattern slipped out of use at the end of the First World War.

Two jacks of the Belgian pattern, which appeared in the middle of the eighteenth century and was derived from the Paris pattern. These cards are significantly different from the French model in one respect—the figures are not named.

Dating from the 1910s, this deck was produced by the Belgian carter Brepols and Diercky Zoon of Turnhout. This town in the Anvers region has been manufacturing playing cards since the eighteenth century, along with its other specialty, printed wallpaper.

Another Belgian pattern,
also derived from the
Paris pattern. However,
this deck has the
particularity of including
a green tone in the
illustration, a color that
is absent from the
French model.

Although these cards with French suit symbols were mostly used in Belgium, they were also exported in considerable quantities to Tunisia and the Italian town of Genoa. That explains why this pattern is often also referred to as the Genoese pattern, or even the Belgian-Genoese pattern.

The playing-card industry of Belgium is nearly as old as that of France. We know of two master card-makers working in Brussels as early as 1427. Later on, Belgian card-makers had their ranks swelled by Frenchmen who, exasperated with the heavy taxes levied on their profession at home, emigrated to Anvers, Bruges and Charleroi.

Although we can trace the adoption by Belgian cardmakers of French suit symbols and face-designs, we do not know exactly when they borrowed the German tradition of highly-decorated aces. Shown here are cards from a so-called "imperial" deck, printed in Belgium for the French market.

Although the production of this card is exquisite, the deck from which it comes is rather curious. Manufactured in Belgium, it has French suit symbols, but the face-designs are from Westphalia—one of the patterns in use in Germany. Moreover, the aces illustrate Napoleon's victories, and the captions are written in French!

Bataille d'Austerlitz 2. Decembre 1805.

Passage du Mont St. Bernard 15 Mai 1800.

... Perhaps the deck is a commemorative one, intended for the inhabitants of Westphalia, a kingdom created by Napoleon in 1807. Or maybe the manufacturer thought that a new and unusual pattern might interest the French public. The lack of corner indices makes it difficult to decide.

A Flemish deck of a rather unconventional pattern, with figures dressed in a style known as "Richelieu." The suit symbols are French, but the corner indices are Flemish, with K (koning) for king, V (vrouw) for queen and B (boer) for jack.

There are some collectors who have an interest not only in the figures presented on cards, but also in the backs of cards, particularly when they display advertising of some description. This Dutch deck was made for a distiller from Schiedam, a major liquor-producing center.

Another advertising deck, this time for Esso. Manufactured in Switzerland, it is functional and bland, aside from the fact that the corner indices are printed on the suit symbols themselves, which is rather unusual.

This deck was manufactured in England for the Belgian branches of the Old England chain of stores, and its back is illustrated with an emblematic Yeoman Warder—who, one might argue, is even more attractive than the figures on the court cards!

Three illustrated aces
depict various famous
Dutch monuments. They
come from a deck produced
in Holland in the second
half of the nineteenth
century. The figures are in
the style of the Frankfurt
pattern; this leads one to
suppose that they were
intended either for export
or else for tourist stores.
Note the rather amusing
style that brings to mind
the Tintin comic strips!

For three hundred years
the crown levied a tax on
decks of cards produced
in England. After 1711 this
tax was levied solely on
the Ace of Spades,
although the reason for
this is unclear. Since then
the card has gone by the
irreverent name of Old
Frizzle. In 1862 the law
changed again, with the
tax being levied solely
on the paper that the
cards were wrapped in.

... With the industry trend towards extravagant visuals, card-makers started to replace the tax seals, which were rather heavy on the eye, with brand emblems that actually were no lighter. Many collectors are interested solely in these Aces of Spades; the oldest of these cards trace the varying rates of tax applied to decks of cards, while more recent ones form a fascinating array of manufacturers. Some of these collectors will willingly break up complete decks in pursuit of their passion.

In France it was the Ace of Clubs that served to display the tax seal, as on this rather well-worn card from a Grimaud deck produced in the 1930s. When the tax was lifted, numerous card-makers replaced the seal with similar round stamps bearing the names of their brands, but not, however, as flamboyant as the decorative stamps of English card-makers.

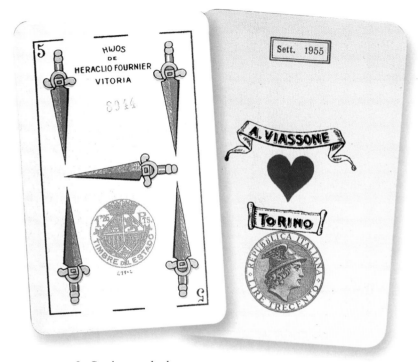

*In Spain, on decks
with Spanish suit symbols, the tax seal appears
on the Five of Swords, while in Italy—where the tax was only lifted in
1972—it was stamped on the Ace of Coins, for decks with Italian suit
symbols. The rule varies for decks with French suit symbols.*

The colors on this deck are wonderfully fresh, despite being over a hundred years old. This is a Hamburg pattern, illustrated by Felix Simon and printed by Chartier, Marteau et Boudin, successors to Grimaud. Note the perforation in the center of the cards, indicating a discarded casino deck.

The Berlin pattern has been in existence since at least the beginning of the nineteenth century and is still used today. In general, German decks do not have queens, and their suit symbols differ from those of the French. So while the Berlin pattern is a derivative of the Hamburg pattern, it has queens, although they do not wear crowns; it also uses French suit symbols.

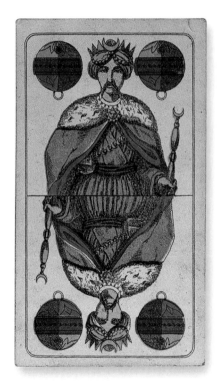

In decks of the Prussian pattern the kings are often accompanied by four pips, in this instance four bells. The figures may be in either double-ended or full-length format. The pip cards are decorated with illustrations of towns or mountains, in the manner of the German decks.

Two lovely pip cards from a late-nineteenth-century pattern coming from Franconia, a region of Bavaria. Note the indication of the number ten with a roman numeral; number indications are absent from cards of lower value.

The Ansbach pattern is one of the oldest known German face-designs. It was still in use in the towns of Ansbach, Nuremberg, Banberg and Würzburg until the 1970s ...

... before being replaced by the Bavarian pattern, examples of which you may find on the following two pages. This deck dates from the 1950s.

Two cards from a recent Bavarian deck on which the suit symbols have been printed in duplicate. In German the bells (schellen) and the acorns (eicheln) have only one nomenclature, while hearts (herzen) may also be called rot (red) and the leaves laube or grün (green).

One of the characteristics of the Bavarian pattern is the depiction of a young boy sitting on a barrel, holding a glass. In older decks the child resembles Bacchus. On the card shown here, however, which dates from the end of the nineteenth century, the traditional wine theme has been replaced by that of beer!

The hearts and bells on the first German decks were painted red with black shading; the leaves and the acorns were simply green. Things got more sophisticated as time went by. The acorns became yellow, green and blue, as on these two ober from the Wurtemberg pattern, one of which is an old print and the other a modern one. Try identifying the differences between them. The card on the left is the work of a card-maker from the former East Germany. Perhaps he was a little too stuck in the past!

Dondorf of Frankfurt has produced many decks which have been reprinted countless times. So popular have they become that they are now considered standard patterns. The card pictured here dates from the early twentieth century.

Another Dondorf deck, copied in many countries, including Poland, Austria, Iceland and Denmark, and which dates from the same period. It is often referred to as the "Rhenish pattern," despite the fact that the river that flows through Frankfurt is called the Main!

These cards are from a Trappola deck. The origins of the game itself are lost in time, but we know that the rules of the game are Italian—trappola means "little trap"—and that the design is derived from Venetian decks. Cards like this cropped up in Germanic countries in the seventeenth and eighteenth centuries, with this migration giving rise to variants in the game's rules.

This deck was produced up until the end of the Second World War, particularly in Vienna, Prague and Graz, at the heart of the old Austro-Hungarian Empire. The deck pictured here is a reprint by Ernst Ragg of an original model produced in the nineteenth century by the Viennese card-maker Piatnik.

The Viennese pattern was once widely used across the Austro-Hungarian Empire, as well as in Switzerland and Bavaria. Its use today is generally restricted to Austria and certain regions once belonging to Czechoslovakia.

Apart from the refinement of the clothing—notice the finesse in the drawing of the lace—particularities of the design are the high, flared crowns on the kings, the flat bonnet of the Queen of Hearts, and the roll of parchment clutched by the King of Hearts. This deck from 1971 is the work of the Viennese card-maker Piatnik.

This card comes from a reprint of a Danish deck. Its pattern is called Homblads II, after the name of the card-maker who produced and sold it at the end of the nineteenth century. Active from 1837 to 1890, he produced several designs that have since become standard.

This is a reprint of a Swedish design that was first produced in 1902 by Öbergs of Eskiltuna.

As you will have realized by now in your perusal of this chapter, the Paris pattern was a highly influential one. One of the many designs inspired by it is the Russian one, whose particularities include the turban worn by the King of Diamonds. Note also the face peeking out of the folds of the Queen of Hearts' dress.

The Russian pattern appeared around 1840, but these particular cards date from the second half of the twentieth century and were produced by the card-maker K. M. The corner indices are in Russian; their meaning is given on page 239.

The oldest known deck with a pattern of the seasons comes from the Hungarian town of Pest. Produced around 1835 by Joseph Schneider, it has eight jacks, each bearing the name of a character from Schiller's work *William Tell* (1804), which was performed in Hungary in 1833.

... This makes it the only standard pattern directly inspired by a work of literature. The nameless kings are on horseback, while the seasons are depicted on the daus cards—tavasz *(spring)* on the Deuce of Hearts, nyar *(summer)* on the Deuce of Bells, ösz *(autumn)* on the Deuce of Leaves and tel *(winter)* on the Deuce of Acorns. The cards shown here are from a reprint of 1969.

This card is taken from the reprint of a Bohemian deck produced by the Czech card-maker Obchodni of Kollin. The Bohemian pattern is one of the oldest in the Austro-Hungarian Empire. Many of its particularities are to be found on the pip cards ...

... like the bear leaders on this Ten of Bells. Other interesting vignettes include Eros shooting an arrow on the Ten of Hearts, a flower in a pot on the Sevens of Hearts and of Bells, an elephant on the Eight of Leaves and a pipe smoker on the Seven of Acorns.

The Trieste pattern is the imperial version of the Venetian pattern and was intended for the Adriatic provinces of the Austro-Hungarian Empire. Its suit symbols are those of the Italian decks. In addition to printed maxims, the aces have specific decorations according to suit—clubs are represented by two crescent moons and a cockerel, coins by bunches of grapes, swords by griffins and cups by a three-headed fountain.

The Trieste pattern has been double-ended ever since the nineteenth century. And as in the Venetian pattern, the kings carry lances in addition to their suit symbols. The horses of the Knights of Cups, Clubs and Coins are plumed, unlike the horse of the Knight of Swords, as we see here.

This lovely deck from the end of the nineteenth century has a Greek face-design. It is an example of a real effort to reconcile the tradition of playing cards—hence the French suit symbols—with the culture and traditional costume of the country for which they are destined.

It is most likely that these cards were produced by Grimaud, designer of a similar deck. At the end of the nineteenth century, this card-maker became the official supplier to the Greek government, which then had a monopoly on the sale of this deck.

The Joker

FERD. PIATNIK & SÖHNE, WIEN

The joker is an American invention that dates from around 1860. It was introduced into European decks at the end of the nineteenth century. The joker was created to potentially replace any other card in the deck—in poker it can take any value given to it by the player. In general the joker is represented as a jester, buffoon or court fool. And just as there are collectors whose sole interest is aces (see page 94), so there are collectors whose focus is jokers.

Italy has around twenty regional patterns. It is impossible to determine a precise figure since the criteria for clearly differentiating one design from another vary from specialist to specialist.

The variations introduced by Italian card-makers over time have proved controversial, but they have long provided rich and diverse pickings for collectors. This deck, with a pattern from Piacenza, was produced by Lambissa & Co. in 1929.

Here is a good illustration of what was mentioned on the preceding page. On the left we see a Knight of Coins with the pattern from the Italian town of Trento, a card produced recently by Modiano. According to the conventions of this pattern, the character should be bare headed; as we can see, though, he wears a beret. On the facing page, the left-hand card is the work of the cardmaker Masenghini and depicts a Knight of Cups in the Bergamo style; on the right is a knight in the style of Brescia, produced by Modiano. These patterns from Bergamo and Brescia are generally thought to be local variants on the Trento pattern.

STAB. MODIANO

There are no queens in decks with Latin suit symbols (that is, the symbols used on Italian and Spanish decks). There are knights instead, distinguishable by their horses from the jacks, who go on foot! This Jack and Knight of Clubs are in the Italian regional style from Romagne—which is similar to the French pattern from Plaisance—and come from a deck produced by Viassone in 1970. The card on the far right is of the same pattern and dates from the same year, but is the work of the card-maker Dal Negro.

The pattern from Bologna is very old; in the early full-length versions a servant figure was depicted where later one would see the Jack of Cups. On the Jacks of Clubs and Swords there appeared the inscriptions Libertas and Bologna, respectively. With the switch to double-ended designs these particularities were lost. The card pictured here is from a deck produced by Modiano in the 1970s.

A Four of Cups from a 1973 reprint of a deck in the style of the Italian town of Viterbo. The pattern dates from 1855 and was inspired by the designs from Romagne and Plaisance; on older decks the she-wolf who suckled Romulus and Remus appeared on the Four of Coins. The deck from which this card comes was perhaps an attempt to revive this pattern, which disappeared after the Second World War.

These two cards are from
a Venetian deck bearing
the Italian suit symbols—
swords (spadi), clubs (battoni),
cups (coppe) and coins
(denari). A particularity of
this deck is the presence
of maxims on the aces.
Note the similarity between
this Ace of Swords and the
Trieste pattern on page 122.

Another particularity is that the Jack of Swords is depicted as an executioner with a head impaled on the end of his sword. The Venetian pattern is the oldest one in Italy to have been designed double-ended but bisected horizontally. This deck was produced and sold by Dal Negro of Treviso between 1972 and 1988.

In very old Florentine decks three distinct patterns were used. In the course of the nineteenth century the Tuscan pattern was born from these three, however its use was quite limited.

Not only are the cards of the Tuscan pattern shorter than other Italian cards, but they use French suit symbols; the Jack of Clubs carries a large book, while the King of Hearts either reads or holds a parchment, which is sometimes sealed, sometimes not. Note the cleverness of the card-maker Viassone, who has used these two objects to advertise his name! This deck dates from 1955.

Another Italian deck with French suit symbols is the pattern from the Lombardia region, sometimes called the Milanese design. Although it is a very old design, it bears many similarities to French illustrated decks, except that the double-ended court cards are bisected horizontally.

This King of Diamonds would appear to be following the example of the King of Hearts from the Lyon pattern, who was also depicted with a parrot. Another element of interest is the Milanese coat of arms that appears on the Jack of Clubs. This deck dates from the 1960s and is the work of the card-maker Dal Negro.

It is not only because of its French suit symbols that the Piedimonte pattern is very similar to the Paris pattern, brought to Italy in the eighteenth century. But despite the Italian card-makers'— here the work is by Dal Negro—taking their inspiration from their French colleagues, they did not bisect their double-ended court cards diagonally.

There exist decks with the Piedimonte pattern from the early nineteenth century in full-length format, but they all became double-ended between 1820 and 1830. Some elements of the official French pattern of 1813 still remain, like the cockerel in the folds of the King of Diamonds' cloak (see page 64) or the eagle in that of the Queen of Spades.

The Sicilian and Sardinian (facing page) patterns are derived directly from Spanish decks, doubtless due to Spain's sovereignty over these two islands in the fifteenth century. The pip cards are often decorated with little motifs; sometimes the face of Garibaldi appears on the Five of Coins. This deck was produced by Pignalosa of Naples.

This deck is the work of Dal Negro, a card-maker since 1928. The Sardinian pattern is directly inspired by a deck produced in Madrid in 1810 by Clemente Roxas. The background to the full-length figures is often illustrated with a landscape or theatrical scene. Figures from the sword suit are depicted wearing armor, as this jack demonstrates.

Although Spanish decks have evolved over time, they use the same suit symbols as Italian decks. Theories abound as to how these symbols made their way to Spain. One strong possibility is that they were brought by papal soldiers who had followed Du Guesclin in his campaign against Peter the Cruel in 1367. These cards were printed by Sebastien Comas y Ricart in 1850.

The Spanish suit symbols are cups (copas), coins (oros), clubs (bastos) and swords (espadas). Although Spanish card-makers took much of their inspiration from Italian cards, they also introduced colors that did not appear in Italian decks, particularly this very bright blue, but also some lovely rich orange tones (see page 146).

Suits are identifiable not only by their symbols, but also by the lines that run along the top, bottom and sides of the cards and which are interrupted different numbers of times according to the suit—once for cups, twice for swords, three times for clubs and none for coins. The two cards shown on these pages come from a deck produced by Alami in Casablanca, Morocco.

During the second half of the nineteenth century the Basque card-maker Heraclio Fournier oversaw the creation of the Castilian pattern that would later be copied by all Spanish card-makers.

These two Knights of Clubs are the work of Heraclio Fournier of Vitoria. The card on the left is a reprint from an 1868 deck that was unveiled at the Paris Exhibition of the same year. The other card comes from a deck that was on sale between 1920 and 1940. Notice the way the horse walks backwards; this is considered one of the particularities of the Castilian face-design.

According to Gwenael Beuchet of the Musée Français de la Carte à Jouer, "Baptiste-Paul Grimaud is the perfect example of the famous stranger." His name has graced thousands of decks of cards since 1851. Born to a family of modest means, Baptiste-Paul Grimaud forged his career as a card-maker over fifty years, creating a huge empire and acquiring a virtual monopoly over the production of playing cards in France.

Apart from the numerous patents that he registered, and which then became benchmarks for the profession, he also directed his efforts towards the export market. The Grimaud firm was eventually taken over by France Cartes, which continues to use the brand to this day. The cards shown here are from a Spanish deck and date from the 1910s.

Although the ace bears the inscription "Fabrica d'Anton Llombart, Barcelona, 1824," the deck that these two cards come from was printed for the Spanish market by the Marseille manufacturer Levenque, who bought the original woodcuts. There exist many other examples of this type of transaction, for the Mediterranean card-makers produced much work for the Spanish.

The practice was not limited to the Mediterranean, though. Jehan Volay, the famous card-maker from Thiers, produced decks for export featuring the Auvergne pattern, but with Spanish suit symbols!

To each era its style. This King of Swords is a 1977 reprint of a Spanish neo-classical pattern from Madrid, engraved and hand-painted in 1810 by Don José Martinez de Castro. The card on the right comes from a Nacional deck by Heraclio Fournier.

Each card in a Spanish deck has a number in its top-left and bottom-right corners that indicates its value. So this king is the twelfth card in its suit and not the thirteenth, since these Spanish decks do not have a number ten. Decks for one of the most popular national games, Hombre, do not even have eights or nines.

A very amusing Spanish deck intended for Egypt. Note how the Knight of Cups has been given an Eastern look. Los Dos Tigres is a brand of the card-maker Heraclio Fournier. It appears on the Ace of Coins, in the place where the Spanish coat of arms was printed on many older decks.

Figures in Spanish decks appear in full-length format, as they do in certain German decks and many Italian ones. The major problem with this format is that a player can tell if his or her opponents have one or more court cards when they turn them the right way up in their hands. Naturally, one would expect more experienced players to simply look at them upside down, and thus avoid such a disadvantage. This problem disappeared with the advent of double-ended court cards.

Today we are used to decks of playing cards having a variety of decorations on their backs. However, this is quite a recent phenomenon. On the oldest decks the backs of the cards were plain. Gradually they were decorated with small, simple motifs, either geometric or repetitive. It was the arrival of offset printing in 1900 that allowed for elaborate, multi-colored designs. One often wonders, though, why card-makers do not make more use of them to advertise their brands.

15.T.88.1174

Dating from the end of the nineteenth century, these two cards are the work of the Lisbon card-maker Real Fabrica and are characteristic of the Portuguese pattern, with this strange character on the Two of Clubs ...

... and an Ace of Cups that is decorated with a dragon. The other three aces feature dragons as well; hence the colloquial reference to the Portuguese deck as the Dragon Deck. The oldest Portuguese deck dates from 1597 and was produced by Pietro Ciliberto.

Although this deck was printed by Litografia Maia of Porto in the second half of the twentieth century, an identical deck appeared in the catalogue of the German card-maker Dondorf between 1889 and 1933.

However, the deck was identified by M. Thissen—who donated a collection containing it to the Musée Français de la Carte à Jouer—as being a Portuguese pattern. Until further research bears fruit, let us simply admire these medieval characters and the aces with their airy, floral decoration.

Despite their Latin suit symbols, these cards are French, and were used for the game of Aluette. This is a very old game whose origins are unknown, but traces of it go back as far as the fifteenth century, when it was played by French and Spanish sailors. A game lasts five rounds, and the aim is to take as many tricks as possible. To take a trick one has to beat the other players' highest card, and to do this it is necessary to know the strength of these other hands. However, the value of the cards cannot be conveyed verbally ...

... *players have to use mime to tell not only their opponents what hands they have, but their partners too. Which is all the charm of the game. Some of the sign language is conventional, some of it made up on the spot by the players. The cards pictured here are from a modern Aluette deck produced by Grimaud.*

*In the game of Aluette,
the Two of Clubs is also called the deux d'écrit or
"two of writing," because it cites the name of the
card-maker. This card dates from 1860 and was
produced by the Bruneteau of La Rochelle.*

Aluette is also called *Jeu de la Vache* or the Cow Game, a reminder of which is the back of this card. The cow, along with Monsieur or Madame Borgne (Mr. or Mrs. One-eyed), represents one of the strongest cards.

This card is from the French Tarot Federation's official deck. Called the "New" Tarot (see page 343), it is largely derived from a deck produced by the German Wüst firm of Frankfurt around 1865. The suit symbols are French, and a knight is added to the three traditional court figures of each suit. The trump cards depict various scenes from daily life ...

... which, despite a few liberties being taken with the original, are quite faithful to their German model. The appearance of this Grimaud deck on the French market triggered a renewed interest in the game of Tarot in France.

In addition to Tarot, the Germans have another game called Cego. It is played with a Tarot deck minus twenty-four cards. There are two known models of the Cego deck: an animal or Adler-cego, and a Cego from the Black Forest which is similar to the New Tarot mentioned on the preceding page. The deck from which this card comes was produced recently in Stuttgart by VASS, and uses nineteenth-century illustrations.

These Japanese cards, called mekuri or tenshu cards, are in fact derived from Portuguese cards introduced to Japan in the sixteenth century. Despite several prohibitions they have managed to survive by using local designs and colors. The court cards are all there—kings (kiri or koshi), knights (uma or muma), queens that are called "servants" or "foreigners" (sôta) and aces with dragons (robai).

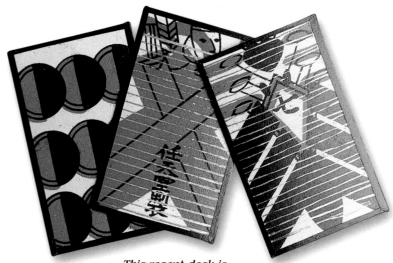

*This recent deck is
produced by Nintendo Playing
Cards of Kyoto, and features Napoleon
Bonaparte on the deck's wrapper.*

G A M E

*Like the cards on the preceding two pages,
these Kabu cards are derived from
Portuguese decks of the sixteenth century.
They differ, however, in that they are ordered
into three suits with identical card values, to
which is added a suit of varied cards. The card
on the left is from the coins suit.*

Kabu cards have several regional models. This so-called Kudosan ("mountain of the nine weathers") deck is characteristic of the Kyoto region and western Japan. It is produced by Nintendo, the same company now known all over the world for its video games!

These are perhaps not traditional playing cards at all, since they bring to mind the pieces for the banking game Tehonbiki, in which a "banker" selects a card from one to six and the player has to guess which card has been selected. The complete set consists of seven identical suits of six cards.

These particular Japanese cards are here reproduced at full size. You can see how much smaller they are than Western cards, as well as being printed on a much thicker cardboard.

 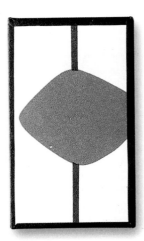

*Hana Funda, or the "game of flowers," comprises
six suits of four cards, each one corresponding
to a month of the year and to a flower. No
indication of their value is given; the player is
supposed to deduce it from the illustration.*

Unlike the major games played in Japan—Go, Shogi and Mah-jong—which are of Chinese origin, the Game of Flowers is typically Japanese. The producer of these cards was probably Nintendo, which was founded in 1933 and made only playing cards until the 1950s, when it diversified into other games.

A bit of roundness in a rectangular world!
And all thanks to these Indian cards whose
suits illustrate the ten incarnations of
Vishnu. Each of these two kings is a
representation of this divinity.

Apart from the kings (raja) on the facing page, this deck is composed of ministers (mantri) and ten numbered cards, each illustrating a different theme.

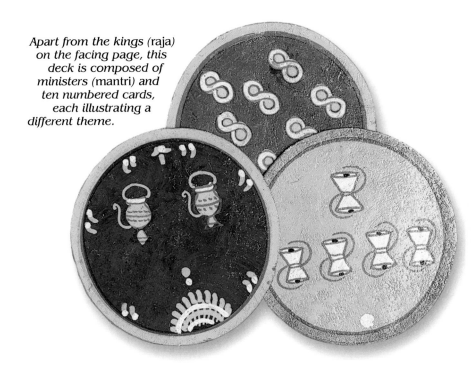

Traditional Indian decks of cards (ganjifa) illustrate the ten incarnations (avatara) of Vishnu and are commonly called Dasavatara Ganjifa. But European playing cards have been so popular on the subcontinent ...

... that traditional cards have had English pips added to them. This makes for some curious mixes; for example, here the Nine of Clubs is illustrated by the god Jagannath.

In 1565 Abdul Fazil, vizier and biographer of the
Mongol emperor Akbar the Great, described various decks
of cards. One of these was the Moghul Ganjifa, composed
of eight or twelve suits of twelve cards each, including a
king and a minister, and ten pip cards. The illustrations
were based on military, animal and mythological motifs.

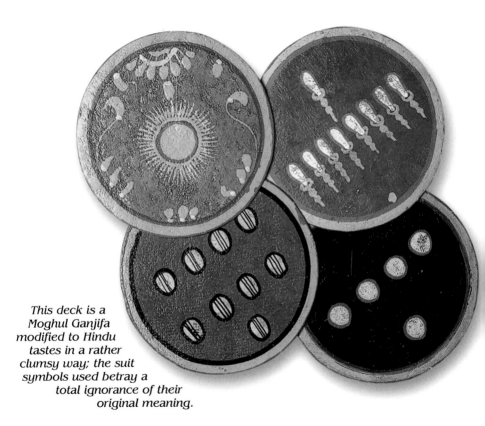

This deck is a Moghul Ganjifa modified to Hindu tastes in a rather clumsy way; the suit symbols used betray a total ignorance of their original meaning.

European cards were introduced to the Indian subcontinent during the colonial period. The wealthier classes were quick to demand cards with European suit symbols, which were nevertheless illustrated in a local manner.

And so these kinds of decks were born, many of them produced in Orissa, the only region in India where cards are still made by hand. These cards date from the 1960s.

These recently printed cards are from Borneo and form part of a Phai Phong deck. There are 116 of them, and they are divided into two suits, one black and one white, each of which is divided into six suits of eight identical cards and one suit of ten identical cards. These fourteen suits represent the pieces of Chinese chess—general, mandarin, elephant, horse, war engine, canon and foot-soldier.

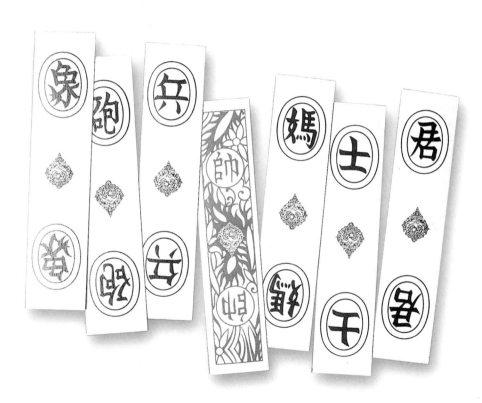

This deck is a transposition of Chinese dominoes into cards, produced by the Guan Huat Company of Hong Kong. It is composed of two suits of

twenty-one cards with pips
indicating different values.
The illustrations are purely
decorative or symbolic. Certain
decks have even been adorned
with portraits of theater actors.

The origin of these monetary cards is an amusing one. The sapeque, a currency used in China and Indochina, was once so weak that for ease of use the coins, which were perforated, were strung on rings. Someone had the bright idea of reproducing this on paper, thus creating the

*Suits (100 to 900 sapeques), the Ciotta (10,000 to
90,000 sapeques) and the Myriads (100,000 to 900,000
sapeques). This was how the game of Kan Hu was born,
among others. Shown here is a recent deck produced
by Pura Dewa, a card-maker from Southeast Asia.*

II

PICTORIAL
playing cards

The cards in this collection are particularly inventive and the card makers have given full reign to their creativity and ingenuity, replacing traditional figures—and sometimes even the suit symbols—with characters from history, contemporary events or their own imagination. Hundreds of these kinds of illustrated decks have been produced, and the trend is still going strong, for the cardmakers of today are well aware of the size of the collector's market. Although some of these decks have been more appreciated than others, none of them are ever boring! And you will find some real curios towards the end of the chapter—examples of marked and other special cards, designed for use by conjurers and other card "pros."

Some of the most famous illustrated decks were produced by the German card-maker Johann Friedrich von Cotta— founder of the Allgemeine Zeitung and other newspapers. Apparently he was inspired to pursue this creative line by the growth of illustrated calendars in Germany and France.

This deck dates from 1811 and depicts representatives of the various orders of knights. The card on the left shows the Order of the Crescent, that on the right the Order of Saint Lazare. Other orders illustrated include the Order of the Elephant and the Order of the Templars. But for a change, the court cards are not the most amusing!

Bearing absolutely no relation to the cards on the preceding pages, despite being part of the same deck, the pip cards depict scenes of daily life.

*These cards are called Comic Karten in
Germany, while in English they commonly
go by the name of "transformation decks."
The way in which the suit symbols are
integrated so seamlessly into the illustrations
is a marvel to behold.*

The first of von Cotta's decks appeared in 1805; its figures are inspired by Schiller's play about Joan of Arc, Die Jungfrau von Orleans. It was illustrated by the countess Charlotte von Jennisson-Walworth, as was the deck shown here, which is von Cotta's last and dates from 1811. There is a total of five von Cotta transformation decks, every card of which is different.

The six von Cotta cards reproduced in these pages all come from the same deck, that of 1811. They are all etchings, water-colored by hand. This deck was very successful and sold widely in France, notably in Paris.

Other card-makers were greatly inspired by the success and ingenuity of the von Cotta decks. This card is a color lithograph produced by Grimaud between 1851 and 1866. Illustrated by Le Tellier, the card measures six inches by three inches, which is larger than average and accentuates the effect of looking at a small painting.

Most of the characters featured in these decks are purely fictional. The comportment of this King of Clubs is quite un-royal. This deck is often called the Jeanne Hachette deck, for the Queen of Spades (reproduced on page 196 at the beginning of this chapter) is considered to be a representation of the French heroine who defended Beauvais from the besieging army of Charles the Reckless in 1472.

As is the case with the von Cotta deck, the pip cards of
the Jeanne Hachette deck bear no resemblance to
the court cards. But whereas the suit symbols of
the von Cotta deck were added by hand, in watercolor,
those of the Hachette deck were printed at
the same time as the rest of the scene.

It is understandable that artists should wish to avoid the rigid and conventional manner in which suit symbols are traditionally depicted, and to turn this constraint into a source of inspiration. Their efforts are highly inventive and extremely charming.

Here are two more lovely cards from the same deck as those on the two preceding pages. In 1870 the German cardmaker Fromme und Bunte of Darmstadt produced a copy that it called not Jeanne Hachette, but Jeanne d'Arc, or Joan of Arc.

To make matters even more complicated, this was not a copy of the original, but a copy of a copy of the original that had been produced not long before by Braun & Schneider! This may explain why these decks have sometimes been confused with each other.

This deck was produced by the United States Playing Cards Company in 1895 in Cincinnati. Despite being called Vanity Fair n° 41, it was in fact the first illustrated deck produced by this American card-maker. Apart from the charming transformed pip cards (facing and two following pages), the traditional figures on the court cards are given a humorous touch—notice the eye-patch on the King of Clubs and his rough bludgeon instead of a scepter!

In England and America, these transformation cards are called comic or Harlequin cards, terms also used occasionally in France.

*If ever you should be tempted to start
collecting decks of comic cards, Germany,
Austria, Great Britain, the United States and
France have produced sixty such decks
between them, whereas Italy has only ever
produced one, called Album. Poland also
has but a single comic deck.*

Serious collectors should forget about the commercial comic decks and go for those unique, hand-produced editions. For when the vogue for decks of comic cards was at its peak, many artists took up their brushes to produce decks as singular as any painting. It is said that the nineteenth-century English novelist William Thackeray liked to amuse himself with just this hobby.

Of similar spirit to the decks produced during the French Revolution (see pages 58 to 63), in 1848 the card-maker Lartigue produced a set of Republican Cards, also known as the Liberators' Deck, of which this card is an example. The kings are Napoleon Bonaparte, George Washington, William Tell and Simon Bolivar. A small sword is placed beneath the suit symbol on the king cards so they will not be confused with the jacks, who have a little flag there instead.

The queens follow the same logic, representing Liberty, Equality and Fraternity, while the Queen of Clubs represents the Republic. Notice the outline of the Palais Bourbon, or Bourbon Palace, in the background, seat of the Assemblée Nationale, which here bears its truncated inscription. Grimaud produced a reprint of this deck in 1985.

This deck of "Indian cards" was the product of the fascination with all things Oriental that was fashionable at the start of the twentieth century. The deck was produced by Grimaud, the same card-maker who had registered a patent in 1877 to place suit symbols in the corners of playing cards (K for king, Q for queen, J for jack) or a number to indicate value (in the case of the pip cards). This innovation allowed players to keep their cards close together, thus minimizing the risk of cheating. You only need to look at any modern playing card to see the success of his system! This deck has not yet received such indices.

This deck of the Four Continents was
illustrated by Friedrich Karl Haussmann and dates from the early
twentieth century. Notice the beautiful back, depicting Fortune
borne across the world on a globe, scattering flowers.

Color lithographed by Dondorf, each of the suits in this deck is devoted to a continent—clubs for America, hearts for Asia, spades for Africa and diamonds for Europe. Each card, including the pip cards, bears a different illustration, most of them evoking fauna and flora, like this Ten of Clubs. At the bottom of the card is the inventory number of the Musée Français de la Carte à Jouer (see page 368), to whose collection it belongs.

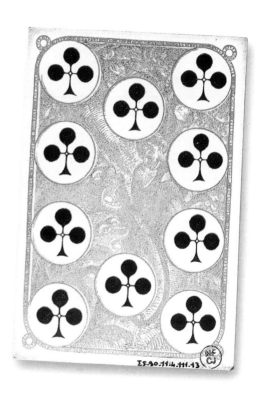

Commonly called Paleh, this lovely Russian deck with its black background was printed for the first time by the Muscovite card-maker Gosudarstvennoi in 1939. These cards come from a 1967 reprint, probably made to celebrate the 150th anniversary of another card-maker, Leningradskii Kombinat, of Saint Petersburg.

This luxurious deck of cards was printed in 1897 by Chas Goodall & Co. Ltd of Old Bond Street, London, to celebrate the sixtieth year of Queen Victoria's reign. On the back of each card appears an illustration of the queen, based on a photograph taken by Bassano. The court cards depict English monarchs from the Plantaganets to the Tudors, Stuarts and Hanovers.

This German deck from the nineteenth century illustrates the Leipzig fair, a popular event, celebrated since the fifteenth century, that takes place each January, Easter and autumn, attracting a clientele from all over Europe. It is a major trading center for furs, textiles and porcelain.

Indeed, a fur trader is featured on both the card on the left and the one on the right, along with a young woman dressed in the costume of the Attenberg region, a postman in his yellow uniform and even a Greek proudly wearing his national dress!

Swiss culture was very much in vogue during the second half of the nineteenth century, so it became necessary to satisfy the demands of the accompanying tourist market. The backs of the cards in this deck each depict different Swiss landscapes. As for the figures, they are dressed in traditional costumes from different cantons, whose flags appear opposite the suit symbols.

So popular were these cards that, according to hearsay, the canton of Geneva—whose urban style was based upon those of Paris and whose peasant costumes resembled those of the nearby Dauphiné region—actually invented a costume so as not to be left out! This delightful deck is the work of the card-maker Müller of Schaffhouse, and dates from 1870. Illustrated by Graf and colored by hand, the cards are shorter and wider than normal.

With the Republic of Ireland having been established in 1921 following the Treaty of London, this deck from the 1930s might be seen as an attempt to create a national pattern to compete with the English design. But players' habits were stronger.

Laegaire (on the left) is one of Ireland's legendary Celtic heroes; the Jack of Hearts (on the right) holds a harp, one of Ireland's national symbols.

This Belgian deck illustrates the world of horse-racing. The aces depict views of race courses, while the court cards portray jockeys on horseback. The kings' cards feature suit symbols surmounted by crowns so as not to be confused with the jacks.

Rennplatz von Baden-Baden

The town of St. Hubert
in Belgium has long
played a key role in
hunting in continental
Europe. This St. Hubert
deck dates from 1956
and depicts hunting
scenes. Everything is
included, from hunting
attire to bugling to a
wild boar felled by a
spear. The cards
reproduce watercolors
painted by Eugène
Lelièpvre and were
printed in Paris
by Philibert.

Notice how these cards are larger than normal and how well the artist has succeeded in his depiction of the double-ended queen—the horse's neck blends wonderfully into the skirts of its lady rider.

This astounding Italian deck, called Italia Nuova, dates from the time of Mussolini. Produced by R. Pignalosa fu Luigi of Naples, it was very probably printed at the end of the 1920s. Notice the back (facing page, right), which is an allegory of Italy, depicting each of the suit symbols reproduced on the pip cards.

This German deck—the Seven and King of Bells are reproduced here—illustrates the exploits of German aviation from 1914 to 1918. Each of the face cards depicts an officer or a pilot who had distinguished himself in the service. It is a very masculine world, which is appropriate when you remember that German decks have no queens!

Another era, but also a military theme.
This time it is the French Foreign Legion that is
depicted, in illustrations by Rosenberg.
The deck was produced by Polaires of Nice. Each
card is different, but once again the male rules,
for the queen cards all depict lusty soldiers!

Each suit of this Russian deck, illustrated by Victor Svechnikov and printed in 1971 in St. Petersburg, evokes an opera, including Othello *and* Faust. *The corner indices are in Russian, with the K here indicating* karol *(king).*

This deck dates from 1955; it is illustrated by Paul-Émile Bécat and printed by Philibert. Known as the Florentine, it takes its inspiration from works by Renaissance masters that were destroyed by Savonarole, a severe critic of the morals of his contemporaries.

Detailed descriptions of the paintings survived, however, providing enough information for the artists to create these miniatures. The mood of the deck is gay and frivolous. This Ace of Hearts depicts love, while the King of Clubs depicts Laurent the Magnificent, protector of the arts, in the company of two charming ladies.

This chromolithographed deck was produced by the German firm Dondorf at the end of the nineteenth century. Dondorf of Frankfurt was active from 1858 to 1933.

The characters here are dressed in Louis XIII costume. Notice both the pose of the lady gracing the Queen of Diamonds and the French suit symbols.

These large American cards tell the story of the colonization of America. The back depicts the American eagle (facing page, right). The pip cards bring to mind the German decks with their depiction of the daily activities of both natives and colonizers. The deck was illustrated by David Bloch and printed by Morgan Press in the second half of the twentieth century.

© D. L. Bloch

*Illustrated with green-tinted period photographs,
this luxurious gilt-edged deck was a souvenir
available in California in 1913. It was produced
by M. Rieder of Los Angeles. Each card is different.
This Three of Diamonds shows a view of Palm Drive
in winter—it certainly looks very tempting.*

Some cards are not without a touch of humor, like this donkey that, the caption explains, is having a good laugh waiting for the next new arrival to turn up. Notice the pretty nasturtiums on the back of the card.

INDIAN CHILDREN.

Another deck illustrated with photographs, but this time from Canada. It dates from the beginning of the twentieth century and was produced by the London card-maker Goodall & Sons. Each illustration is different. Notice the very attractive back (facing page, right) showing the coats of arms of all the Canadian provinces, and the emblematic maple leaf and beaver.

SOUS LE CAP STREET, QUEBEC

Produced in 1973 by Soul-Mar Inc., this deck was intended to propagate the beliefs of the Black Panthers, the self-defense organization founded in 1966 by black revolutionary militants claiming "black power." The closed fist raised high appears on the Ace of Spades and the four kings. The joker on the facing page is also very evocative, while the colored costumes and the flowers grasped by the queens call to mind the hippy movement.

Perhaps it is because they weren't involved in the development of the standard pattern that Americans feel that they have a certain freedom to parody traditional playing cards. Produced by Tiffany & Co. of New York, this deck, with its grotesque characters, is a very amusing one.

Notice that the characters are shown full-length and not double-ended; and despite the elements of pastiche—the pot of jam grasped by the King of Hearts or this Jack of Diamonds' memo—the pose of the characters is really quite close to traditional playing cards, such as those presented at the beginning of the GAME chapter.

Here is another pictorial American deck, where the cards are cut obliquely. They sit quite comfortably in the hand, but are rather odd to play with.

Apart from their flesh-colored faces, these figures conform to the traditional English design. This deck was produced by E. Z. Playing Cards of Quincy, Massachusetts.

No, neither the page nor the illustration have been crumpled—these cards really are shaped like this. The Americans call this a crooked deck. Unfortunately, not only are they rather impractical to play with, but you run the risk of becoming a little dizzy, particularly after a hard night playing poker!

For this El Ferrocarril deck produced in Mexico in the second half of the twentieth century, the figures have been given a healthy dose of local color. This rider wears a sombrero, while the young woman dressed in local costume (facing page) provides a most attractive replacement for the jack.

The suit symbols, particularly cups (left) and coins, have also been redrawn in an "Aztec" style. The Ace of Coins in this deck produced by La Cubana is a reminder that the company won a prize at the World Exhibition in Saint Louis in 1904.

K
♥

RICHARD I
1189 - 1199

♠
K

*Here we find quite
a different style, a
deck made by the British
Heritage Playing Card
Company. Founded
in 1993, Heritage soon
conquered the market at
museums, castles and other
historical sites, with its
cards depicting English
monarchs. Since then
it has widened its range
still further (see pages
324 to 329), creating a
collector's goldmine.*

2 ♣

HENRY III
1216 - 1272

ELIZABETH II
1952 -

Habit de Pescheur

This deck is inspired by famous eighteenth-century engravings by Nicolas de Larmessin portraying various trades; the figures sport a variety of work clothes and tools in use in their various guilds.

Although based on prior documents and artwork, this deck, which was produced by the French firm Dusserre, is actually an original design. The firm also produces many exciting reprints, enabling collectors to discover old decks that would otherwise be quite hard to find.

The illustrator and manufacturer of this recent deck are unknown. Printed on un-laminated cardboard in Guatemala, each card depicts a Mayan divinity. The pip cards and backs are also illustrated in the same style.

ARIKI TAPAIRU

ARIKI TAPAIRU

Another recent deck, this one comes from New Zealand; its figures represent imaginary Maori kings and queens.

Conceived and illustrated in 1935 by Molné, this Catalonian deck is called Visca la Sardana. It was produced by the great Basque card-maker Fournier. The traditional suit symbols have been adapted somewhat—the cups transformed into wine decanters and the swords into sickles.

This recent Spanish deck is called Baraxa Galega and depicts Galician culture. Galicia is not one of the three regions that gave rise to the traditional Spanish face-designs: Andalucia, Càdiz and Castile. Interestingly, the costume of this bagpiper resembles that from the French region of Brittany.

*Produced by Dusserre and
called Provinces of France, this deck is a real feast for
lovers of traditional costumes. Eighteen of them are represented
on the kings, queens, jacks and jokers.*

R ♠

LOIRE-ATLANTIQUE

R ♥

PAYSAN D'ESCOUBLAC

Although there are many souvenir decks where the representation of local costumes leaves a lot to be desired, here the authenticity is faultless. This deck of Picturesque Brittany is illustrated in watercolor by François-Hippolyte Lalaisse, who traveled the roads of the region between 1843 and 1844 sketching the local characters.

Quite apart from their sociological interest, these cards are really quite beautiful. There are twenty-two such scenes to admire, since all of the court cards, the jokers and the tens are illustrated. As for the pip cards, they depict some of the sights of Brittany. This lovely collector's deck is the work of Dusserre.

- **271** -

Passengers traveling with Air Afrique thirty years ago received this special deck, where the kings, queens and warriors on the court cards are dressed in traditional African costume. Created by Cedia of Abidjan, these cards were printed in Turnhout, Belgium.

Produced in Ethiopia to order for the Habtezgui family, these cards depict Ethiopian kings, queens and warriors and were published in the second half of the twentieth century.

This deck, printed in Japan by Nintendo, carries both English and Amharic (Ethiopia's official language) corner indices. Even if such initiatives are rarely a commercial success, attempts to adapt face-designs to cultures where cards do not have any historical roots have something touching about them. And of course they are a boon for collectors.

Some of the most inventive decks have been dreamt up by artists. This deck is the work of Charles Pasino, a painter, engraver and poster artist who developed a passion for playing cards that he made himself using traditional craft techniques. These cards date from 1983 and are woodcut prints colored by stencils.

Charles Pasino's jokers are two mandrakes, considered in the Middle Ages to be magical plants and whose root resembles the human body. The Queen of Diamonds on the facing page is the fairy Mélusine. Her bare breasts are not simply twentieth-century provocation; certain queens were depicted like this in decks of old.

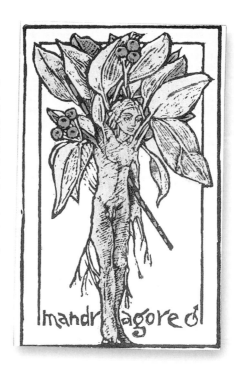

A modern version of the Swiss national pattern and the work of Egbert Moehnsang from 1982. The design might not please everyone, but specialists affirm that, though it has been radically changed, its original spirit has been respected. Shown are the Under and the Eight of Coins.

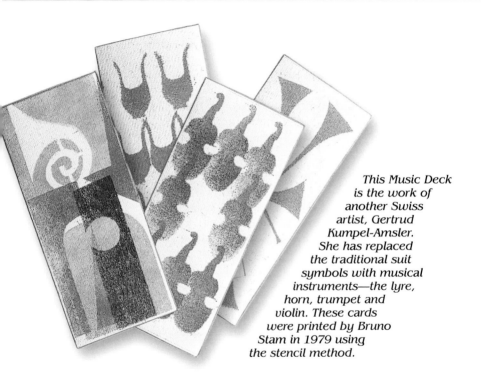

This Music Deck
is the work of
another Swiss
artist, Gertrud
Kumpel-Amsler.
She has replaced
the traditional suit
symbols with musical
instruments—the lyre,
horn, trumpet and
violin. These cards
were printed by Bruno
Stam in 1979 using
the stencil method.

Although it is not possible to explain exactly how they work, these strange double cards were used for magic tricks, suggesting different cards depending on how they were held by the conjurer.

Dating from the early twentieth century, this astounding deck was produced by the Parisian card-maker David. These cards must have been part of a larger set, but the Musée Français de la Carte à Jouer has only sevens, eights, nines and tens. Curiously, only the Eight of Hearts is a standard, whole design.

Without betraying the world of magic, suffice to say that rigged decks exist, as with this card ... which is really two in one!

No, this is not a trick photograph. It really is four cards in one. The name of the card-maker of this recent deck is unknown, unless it has magically disappeared!

At first glance, this American deck with English suit symbols appears perfectly normal. And it is, except for the back. For thanks to an ingenious system of markings, invented by the manufacturer De Land, it is possible to determine the position of each card once they have been arranged according to the mnemonic "De Land's Cards Have Superiority," referring to diamonds, clubs, hearts and spades. That done, it is the dials on the back that give the clues: the four large ones indicate the thirteen cards of each suit to be situated; the little dial on the left indicates the card above and the one on the right the card below the cut.

*Don't worry if you don't understand, for the system
is ingenious but complex. That said, examine the
two apparently identical backs and you will notice
tiny differences in their designs. This deck
was sold exclusively to conjurers.*

III

EDUCATIONAL
playing cards

Cards have served not only for playing games but also as precious vehicles for teaching history, geography, heraldry and astronomy, for example. But there is nothing new about this idea of learning through fun; the first educational cards were printed in 1507 by Thomas Murner, a cleric of the Order of Saint Francis teaching philosophy in Krakow. But so effective was his little invention that he was accused of sorcery and narrowly missed being burned at the stake! One may very well consider the Happy Families decks that appeared at the end of the nineteenth century, and which were intended to teach children to associate particular costumes with particular trades, to be the distant ancestors of today's educational cards.

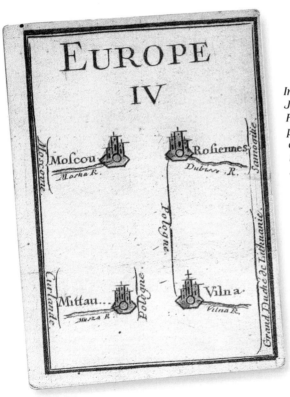

In 1763 Nicolas Jean-Baptiste de Poilly, engraver and printer of educational decks, collaborated with the card-maker Jean-Baptiste Mitoire to produce a deck of geographical cards featuring the four continents of the world: Europe, America, Africa and Asia. (At that time Australia had not yet been discovered by the West).

These cards' suit symbols have been replaced by colors, here yellow. In addition to the kings, queens, jacks, aces and pip cards, there is an additional card featuring a geographical map (like that on page 292).

L'Afrique est presque toute sous la Zone Torride. les Chaleurs y sont Extrèmes. Ses Habitans sont robustes grossiers et farouches. La Terre est assez fertile le long des Costes On y trouve quantité de bons fruits, de

AFRIQUE

Cap. de la MELINDE
Porte de la Coste de Zanguebar.
Mer

Grains, d'Epiceries, de Soyes d'huilles, de Racines, et des Plantes merveilleuses, Il y a dans certains endroits des Mines d'Or et d'Argent. On y trouve toutes sortes d'animaux feroces comme, Lions, Léopards, Panteres, Eléphans, Dromadaires &c.
L'Afrique a donné Naissance à Anibal fameux par les Victoires qu'il remporta sur les Romains.

The pip cards depict a number of towns corresponding to the cards' values, with indications of their region or province, and other information. The commentaries provided to accompany the court cards reveal the received views of the time.
For example, the natives of Africa are described as being "vulgar and savage."

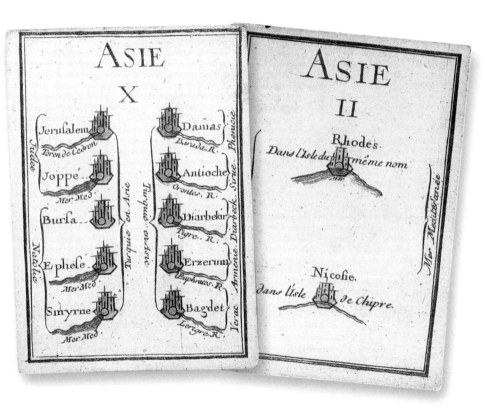

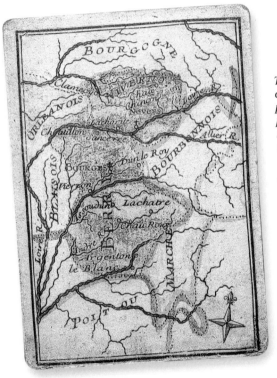

This geographical deck of the French provinces was produced in the same spirit and by the same author as the cards on the preceding pages, Nicolas de Poilly. It contains nine suits of fourteen cards. This is one of the supplementary atlas cards (see page 289).

The known world was described in its entirety in this kind of deck, but not in a balanced manner. France is described in great detail, Europe less so, and the rest of the world much more superficially.

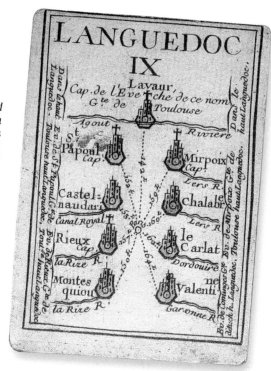

ALEXANDRE, roi de Macédoine. (Grèce)

356 à 323 av. J-CH.

LONGUEURS.

Myriamètre,

10.000 m

One of the results of the French Revolution of 1789 was to introduce the metric system of measurement, in a law dated the 7th of April 1795. Previously, each province—even each region—had its own measures. Often the name of a measure would be the same from one place to another, but the value different!

This deck of cards was produced to help people familiarize themselves with the standard metric system. It must have been a Herculean task, much more difficult than the European Union's recent conversion to the euro, for this was a time not only lacking in calculators and handy converters, but where the majority of the population was illiterate.

This delightful musical deck is identical to one owned by the Bibliothèque Nationale, or National Library of France, and is inscribed with the words "Patented deck. Lith. in color by Boboeuf, rue Cadet, 23." It is accompanied by a document written in calligraphy describing it as a "deck of musical notation" and providing commentaries, diagrams and charts, as well as the rules of the game.

Despite their prime aim being to familiarize card players with musical notation, these cards—produced by Pierre Boboeuf in 1840—also carried traditional card marks so as not to confuse players, as you can see from the Nine of Clubs inset above the sixty-fourth note on the facing page, and the King of Hearts on this page.

Two more cards from the Deck of Musical Notation, but showing actual notes. Apart from the attractive decoration and bright colors, notice the little memory prompt at the bottom of each card.

Pierre Boboeuf also produced arithmetic and alphabet decks. It is very rare to find such decks, particularly complete ones, in secondhand shops; you would have to go to specialist antique dealers and auction houses to get hold of them. But you can always admire them in museums.

A mix of history and imagination, this deck of sovereigns and their mistresses was a great success thanks to the subtlety of its engravings. The court cards depict four kings of France, four ladies who frequented them and four page boys.

Printed as color plates by Chardon, they were turned into a deck of cards by Grimaud in 1856. This particular edition dates from 1858 or later; its corners are rounded, and we know that the patent for this innovation was registered that year.

These cards come from a children's deck produced by Palmier around 1860. All of them are illustrated with different characters or tales. However, the traditional figures and suit symbols also appear in miniature. These cards would have helped introduce children to playing cards by way of a colorful and familiar world, while still being accessible to their parents. Notice the liberty that has been taken with Henri IV as the King of Diamonds (facing page).

This other children's deck
was called Aimez-vous
dans la gloire, or "love
yourselves in glory", and
dates from the end of the
nineteenth century. In the
same spirit as those on
the two preceding pages,
it was produced with
rather more finesse by
Lequart & Mignot.

This Parisian card-maker could be found at 54 rue du Cardinal-Lemoine and was "Successor to Ch. Maurin (previously Maison Arnoult, founded in 1748)." In fact, the original firm of Lequart & Thuillier dates from 1872, becoming Lequart & Mignot in 1878. It was taken over by Grimaud in 1891, who continued to use the brand until 1895.

1. Quand Jean à l'école partait
En l'air toujours il regardait,
Mais il ne s'inquiétait guère
De ce qui se passait à terre.

2. Quand un chien trop vite accourait
Jean, le nez en haut et distrait,
Marchait . . . . au bout d'une minute
Ils faisaient tous deux la culbute!

3. Un jour il descend sur le quai
— Sans même l'avoir remarqué,
Plus qu'un pas — pouff! — dans la rivière
Jean va la tête la première! . . .

The Paul l'Ébouriffé or Disheveled Paul Happy Families deck illustrates nine little fables written by Professor Heinrich Hoffmann and published in 1845. Quite cruel in their way, they take the opposite stance to the moral tales with predictable endings that were legion at the time. This deck was produced by Dondorf and first sold in Germany. So great was its success that it was translated into English and French. Each series consists of four cards. This series tells the tale of John Nose-in-the-Air, who winds up in the river because he doesn't look where he's going. The last card is not shown here, but the story ends thus: "They've fished him out of the water now, / Cold, shaken, and soaking wet, / Pitiful look upon his brow, / Learnt his lesson, that's a bet!"

6

Family MUSTARD-POT (Grocers) THE SON

Famille MOUTARDIER (Épiciers)
LE FILS

Printed several times between 1915 and 1946 by Les Jeux Réunis, this Happy Families deck is really fun; as well as the traditional professions of grocer, cook, cobbler and gardener, it also includes artistic activities.

For example, the Dupinceau or Paintbrush family are all painters, while the Mi-Re-Do family are musicians. The most surprising family is the Trick-Track family. Grandma Trick-Track certainly seems engrossed in whatever card game she is playing! Notice the English translation running up the left-hand side of each card.

This amusing Happy Families deck was produced by Willeb in the 1950s. But it has a unique feature compared to other similar decks—all six cards of a particular family form a frieze, which places the characters in a decor typical of their culture.

FAMILLE PÉKIN

le Grand-père

The Lapp family is depicted on the ice-field, the Nomad family in the middle of the desert and the Senegal family in front of huts and coconut palms. Despite some inevitable clichés, this is a cute way of making children aware that not everybody in the world lives in the same way.

3 FAMILLE HEITZ

LE PERE

The pictures on this Happy Families deck (recently printed by France Cartes) are the work of the great illustrator from Alsace Hansi and would surely delight his many fans. Everything is there, from the night watchman (left) armed with his partisan and carrying his lantern and fog horn, to the characters in traditional costume with geese, kugelhopfs, bottles of riesling and half-timbered houses. It is just a pity that France Cartes did not make more of an effort with the backs of the cards; they are banal, to say the least.

6 FAMILLE UNTERLINDEN

LA FILLE

5 FAMILLE KLEIN

LE FILS

XI. LA RÉPUBLIQUE : HOMMES D'ÉTAT.

Gambetta.
Jules Ferry.
Jaurès.
Clemenceau.

JAURÈS (1859-1914).
Avocat, journaliste, député, grand orateur, il défend les droits des travailleurs.

When I was young I was a mediocre student who had trouble following the school program, which had us switch from antiquity to Napoleon from one year to the next, before returning to Louis IV. So it was not at school that I learned the basics of what today is one of my passions, but through this particular deck of cards. Here we see the Republican statesman Jean Jaurès (1859–1914); lawyer, journalist, member of parliament and orator, he defended workers' rights.

My sisters and I used these cards so much that over time our parents had to buy us at least three decks! This must have made the card-maker Fernand Nathan a tidy profit in the late 1960s. Twelve sets of four cards retrace the history of France. Finally, I could make some sense of my country's history! Here we see Henry IV, King of Navarre before becoming King of France. Tolerant, he accorded the Protestants the Edict of Nantes and developed France's wealth. He reigned from 1589 to 1610.

V. LES GRANDS ROIS.

Henri IV.
Louis XIII.
Louis XIV.
Louis XV

HENRI IV (1553-1610).
Roi de Navarre avant d'être roi de France. Tolérant, il accorde l'Édit de Nantes aux protestants et développe les richesses de la France. (Règne de 1589 à 1610.)

This racist Black Peter deck consists of twenty-five cards. The rules are similar to those for Mistigris—the cards are dealt face-down to the players, who must then make as many pairs as they can, which are then laid face-up on the table. One player asks another player to take a card from his hand and see if he can match it with one of his own. If he cannot, then he must take one from the next player, and so on ...

... until all the cards have been paired. The loser is the player left holding the single card—in this game Black Peter, a little African. The deck was produced by Jean-Pierre Simon France Cartes.

This pairing game was illustrated by the artist James Hodge, author of many other decks of cards. This one, produced by La Ducale, dates from the 1950s and, in addition to its very interesting graphics, is quite amusing. The single card depicts a little clown Ze suis seule ("I'm on my own"), and loses the game for the player left holding it at the end.

... le Gendarme

Decks for Happy Families, pairing games and other cards for children both big and small are a specific collecting theme of their own, so varied are they. They are also interesting since they reveal much about the atmosphere and prejudices of the times in which they were designed.

This fun Indian deck, produced by the Chitrashala Press in Poona, near Bombay, is a real mish-mash of styles as far as the court cards are concerned, with a non-standard face-design repeated in inset on each card, an English index, an illustration of a character, French suit symbols and an inscription in devanagari (the alphabet used for Hindu, Sanskrit and many other Indian languages). The pip cards are illustrated with various objects, including a length of cloth (facing page), a spinning-top, a lotus, a bow and a fish hook. What a blend of cultures! Notice, however, the very European features of the child depicted on the back of the cards.

In 1235 the poet Teika selected 100 poems by 100 different poets, composed between the eighth and twelfth centuries, and wrote them out in beautiful calligraphy. A game developed during the same period, consisting of pairing shells that were first painted with designs, then inscribed with verses from the same poem. Towards the end of the sixteenth century, Teika's collection of poems was transposed onto cards for this very purpose. This game became such a success that its rules grew ever more complex. Since 1951 an annual national championship has been organized in Japan.

河原左大臣（かわらのさだいじん）

みちのくの
しのぶもぢ
摺り誰ゆゑに
乱れそめにし
我ならなくに

ひとつてな
らていふよ
しもかな

4

Thousands of copies of this recent deck are printed today, since all Japanese play the game at least once in their childhood, during the New Year festivities.

3 ♠

3 ♠

♠ 3

♠ 3

Labrador Retriever

With its English suit symbols and corner indices, this deck could fall into the pictorial deck category, except that each card features a different species of dog. Everyone knows the labrador ...

... but how many people know what a Welsh corgi is? Well, the card it is depicted on, the Queen of Spades, provides a clue ... Corgis are the breed favored by Queen Elizabeth II.

Q ♠

Welsh Corgi (Pembroke)

J
O
K
E
R

Diomedea melanophris

Black-browed Albatross
91-96cm

Like the deck featured on the two preceding pages, this deck devoted to sea and coastal birds is produced by Heritage Playing Card Company. Notice that both the common and Latin names of the birds are given, as well as their wingspans.

The same publisher also produces decks devoted to garden birds and water fowl, as well as wild animals, cats, horses, butterflies and fish, to cite but a few.

Fratercula arctica

Puffin
30cm

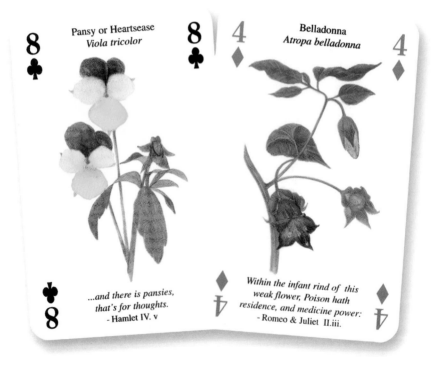

8 ♣

Pansy or Heartsease
Viola tricolor

8 ♣

*...and there is pansies,
that's for thoughts.*
- Hamlet IV. v

♣ 8

4 ♦

Belladonna
Atropa belladonna

4 ♦

*Within the infant rind of this
weak flower, Poison hath
residence, and medicine power:*
- Romeo & Juliet II.iii.

♦ 4

Illustrating a deck of cards with wild flowers (right) is a great idea, but choosing flowers mentioned in the works of Shakespeare and quoting the passage (left) is even better! There is also a deck devoted to plants from the Bible. All of these decks published by Heritage Playing Card Company are available in English, French and German.

Chèvrefeuille des bois
Lonicera periclymenum

To end this chapter, here are three decks that are not strictly speaking educational, but they are special decks that deserve mention. This deck is an Italian Cucco, or "cuckoo," deck. The game is played using two suits of nineteen cards, which are, in order of value, cuckoo, man, horse, cat and inn.

Then follow ten numbered cards, followed by zero, bucket, mask, lion and fool. The rules of the game vary greatly, but the aim is usually to make as many tricks as possible.

Cuckoo games also
crop up in Scandinavia, Germany and Austria, though always in
different forms. This recent deck is a Swedish one and is
published by Esselte Öbergs of Eskiltuna.

Feine Quitli Karten.

This card is from a Quitli deck, a game played by the Jewish communities of Central Europe, and which goes back to the eighteenth century. Some specialists consider it to be a derivative of the Cucco game whose images were removed for religious reasons, while others formally contest this thesis. This recent deck was produced by the card-maker Piatnik & Söhne of Vienna.

PETIT CARTOMANCIEN

49.

Contrarié...
Sépara...
Renver...
Brouille en a...
ou en famil...

RELACHE
CE SOIR

CONTRARIÉTÉ

30

CHANGEMENT

IV

FORTUNE-TELLING
playing cards

O riginating in Italy, the Tarot deck with Latin suit symbols was initially used as a game. The complexity of its rules, varying according to era and region, eventually caused it to fall from favor, and the game of Tarot might well have been lost forever.

But then came the French Revolution, of which one of the most unexpected consequences was the development of an immoderate taste for cartomancy! So it was that the nineteenth century saw a continual growth in the popularity of fortune-telling cards of all kinds, and the Tarot found its place once more. Here is just a small selection of prognostic decks, for no book devoted to playing cards would be complete without them.

The origins of Tarot cards are just as obscure as the origins of traditional playing cards. Because a Tarot deck is composed of a traditional deck with court and pip cards on one hand, and a series of twenty-two trump cards on the other ...

... many people think that
the latter evolved separately
around the fifteenth century.
The two sets would only
have been combined later to
play the game of Tarocchi.
The cards shown here date
from 1842 and are from a
Piedimonte Tarot made by
Gumppenberg.

III

L' IMPERATRICE

This Empress comes from the same deck as the cards on the two preceding pages. The Tarot evokes a very wide range of reactions in people, venerated by some, derided by others.

The Florence Minchiate
is a variant of a traditional
Tarot. One reason for
its slipping out of use
may have been the
number of cards of
which it is composed—
ninety-seven. Among
the cards specific to it
are a cardinal, the four
elements and the twelve
signs of the zodiac ...

... and the three theological virtues of Faith, Charity and Hope, which is the arcanum (Tarot cards are divided into major and minor arcana) shown here.

This card, and those on the two preceding pages, are from the same Minchiate deck from the 1860s. Their back folds over the edges and onto the front, a characteristic of old Italian cards.

This card is from a Bolognese Tarocchino, or Little Tarot, so called because it is missing the twos, threes, fours and fives and so comprises sixty-two cards. Also, two Moors replace the High Priest and Priestess, two cards severely frowned upon by the Church. This deck dates from around 1880; notice the double-ended format.

The fortune-telling Tarot deck uses Italian suit symbols, while the deck used by French players for the game of Tarot Nouveau, or New Tarot, bears French suit symbols (see page 170).

VALET·DE·COUPE

In 1930 Paul Marteau, Grimaud's successor, wanted to market a Tarot deck intended for fortune-tellers. To this end he used the illustrations that Baptiste-Paul Grimaud had found in the Arnoult archives ...

... when he bought Lequart & Mignot (see page 304). And so the "traditional Tarot of Marseille" was born; it is still widely used today. These two cards come from a deck printed in 1969.

The French regional Tarot deck from Besançon is actually a German creation. Due to the Reformation, the Priest and Priestess (Pape, or pope, and Papesse in French) were replaced by Jupiter and Juno. It was only at the beginning of the nineteenth century that this model was produced in Besançon itself, after which it became the sole town to produce it.

It would even appear that there was but a single manufacturer for the deck, one J. Jerger. These two cards from the start of the nineteenth century are his work. This Tarot was published successively by Renault, Kirchner, then Blanche, using the same name, before disappearing. Its only competitor was the Épinal Tarot.

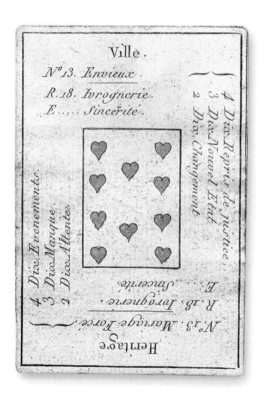

These fortune-telling cards by Saint-Sauveur were inspired by the renowned cartomancer Etteilla, who in the late eighteenth century was at the peak of his fame. The deck comprises thirty of the thirty-two usual cards (reproduced in the center in miniature), to which were added short phrases "enabling the future to be predicted in a convenient manner."

There was an additional card representing "Etteilla, or the questioner." The manufacturer of this deck remains unknown, a sorry state of affairs for a fortune-telling deck! But specialists consider that it dates from 1793. Grimaud has been producing regular reprints of it since the start of the twentieth century, under the name Petit Etteilla.

Known as the Petit Lenormand,
this charming fortune-telling
deck probably dates from the
first half of the nineteenth
century in Germany, Holland
or Belgium. On each card,
numbered from one to
thirty-six, appears an inset
containing an imaginary
character with French suit
symbols, as well as the stamp
of the publisher, Dondorf.
Like many of the other decks
presented in these pages, this
deck is part of the collection
of the Musée Français de la
Carte à Jouer (see page 368).

In the same spirit as the two decks of the preceding pages, this deck by Grimaud France Cartes is a 1994 reprint of the Livre du Destin *or* Book of Destiny, *a nineteenth-century deck.*

Un Jeune Homme brun
A dark haired young Man

Billet doux
Love Letter

In the box containing this deck there is a little booklet explaining the various methods for reading the cards; it affirms that "the reading of the cards should not be considered as a mechanical activity without great significance. That would be to underestimate them and not to read them effectively. For the reading of these cards is as old as playing cards themselves and has always served to announce prophecies."

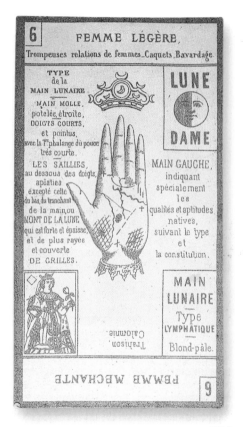

The Deck of the Hand was one of the fortune-telling decks inherited by Grimaud when the company bought the card manufacturer Pussey in 1890. Designed by a certain Adèle Moreau, it is composed of fifty-six cards divided into seven suits of the colors of the rainbow. Palmistry is one of the uses to which this deck may be put, as its name indicates. In addition, the display of the standard cards in a tiny inset means it can be used by people familiar with traditional decks. This deck was reprinted several times by Grimaud, but the cards shown here are from an original model of 1890.

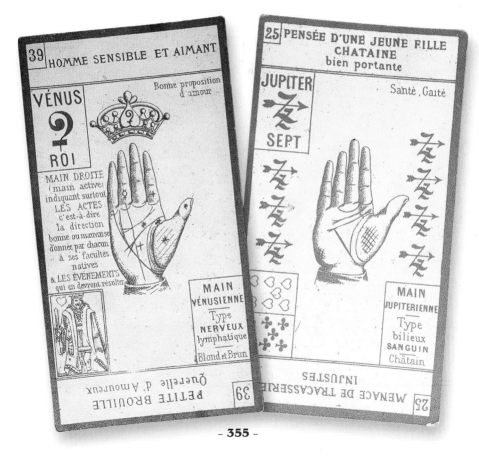

No 3.
Ehestands
karte.

A beautiful German
deck from the start of
the twentieth century.
Like many decks of
this type it is
composed of thirty-
six cards. This one
promises a close
and happy marriage.

This is the card
of hope, as indicated
not only by the
text but by its
symbol, the anchor.
The card-maker
was one Vereinigte
Münchener Spielkarten
of Munich.

Dieťa / Kind
Enfant / Child
18

This Czech deck was designed by Vladimir Tesar in 1967. The illustrations are not without humor ...

... while the captions, printed in Czech, German, English and French, are a great way to brush up on your language skills!

Zlodej / Dieb
Voleur / Thief
30

Printed by France Cartes in 1981, this Tarot was designed by the artist Silvia Maddonni. Taking their inspiration from the Marseille Tarot, the major arcana address the same themes they do in traditional Tarots. Some consider the twenty-two cards to be descended from the twenty-two letters of the original Hebrew alphabet, and to correspond to the twenty-two major arcana of priestly mysticism.

Roy d'Epée
The King of Swords

XX 74

LE JUGEMENT

The artist Éric Provoost has used the myth of the minotaur and the labyrinth to illustrate this 1982 deck. Each card represents one of Theseus's states of mind, as well as the principal themes of the legend. In addition to the corner index, each card bears another serial number, enabling one to follow the story chronologically.

Produced in 2000 by Flammarion 4, this deck by Niki de Saint-Phalle contains only the major arcana of the Tarot. It is accompanied by a booklet in which the artist gives her own

personal interpretation
of each of the cards.
Practitioners of
cartomancy might well
have trouble finding
their way, but it is still
a marvelous collector's
deck!

$$\overline{VI}$$

THE CHOICE

Index, Acknowledgments and Addresses, and Bibliography

Le Musée Français de la Carte à Jouer

I n 1997 Le Musée Français de la Carte à Jouer, or the French
Museum of Playing Cards, moved to its new building, specially
designed to house its collection of playing cards and
numerous related objects. It has a charming atmosphere that is
both cozy and fun. The town of Issy-les-Moulineaux, not far from
Paris, does not itself have a history of playing-card production—
unlike many other towns in the world housing museums devoted
to the subject. In fact, the museum was established following a
donation made in 1930 by a local collector and scholar, Louis
Chardonneret. In 1986 the first exhibition of his personal
collection opened. Over time the museum's collections have been
swelled by acquisitions and new donations. Today it has more
than 6,500 decks, as well as various objects, engravings and
posters. The layout of the museum is stupendous, designed to
protect the cards from the light while providing a very peaceful
setting for the visitor. All year round the museum offers
temporary exhibitions, lectures and workshops for children. There
is also a resource center open to the public, where you may

consult books and other documentation relating to cards and games. Although many of the cards featured in this book come from the museum's collections (you will find a list on page 382), they are not all exhibited permanently. So when you make your visit you will have the pleasure of discovering hundreds of others that you have not seen before!

Reprint by the Viennese card-maker Piatnik of a nineteenth-century Russian Tarot deck. You may find it, along with many other decks, objects and books, at the museum shop, (see address, page 374).

Index

In this index you will find the names of the main publishers, brands, illustrators and printers who are mentioned, or whose work is photographed, in this book.

INDEX

Acknowledgments and Addresses

In particular I would like to thank Monsieur André Santini, mayor of Issy-les-Moulineaux, and Le Musée Français de la Carte à Jouer for the photographic reproductions that they authorized, as well as for all the documentation that was made available to me, which was both abundant and accurate.

Musée Français de la Carte à Jouer
16, rue Auguste-Gervais
92130 Issy-les-Moulineaux
Tel: +33 (0)1.46.42.33.79.
Fax: +33 (0)1.46.45.31.36.
www.issy.com/musee

Thanks are also due to Allan Borvo, a collector of, among other things, playing cards, who was the first person to introduce me to the subject. Thanks also to all the writers who, more or less recently, have written so enthrallingly about playing cards, in particular Thierry Depaulis.

Thank you to my friends Guy Devautour and Anne Chanson.

*And here, for all you card enthusiasts, are a few addresses
of museums that host either permanent or temporary
exhibitions of playing cards.*

The Playing-Card Museum
Beech and Park Streets
Cincinnati OH 45212-3497
United States of America

Belagtingmuseum
Parklaan, 14
1012 RM Amsterdam
Holland

Albertina Graphische Sammlung
Augustinerstrasse, 1
1010 Vienna
Austria

Museo Fournier de Naipes de Alava
Palacio de Bendana
Calle Cuchilleria, 54
01001 Vitoria-Gasteiz
Spain

Nationaal Museum van de Speelkart
Druivenstraat, 18
2300 Turnhout
Belgium

Historiches Museum Basel
Steinenberg 4
4051 Basle
Switzerland

Deutsches Spielkarten Museum
Schonbuchstrasse, 32
Postfach 10 03 51
70771 Leinfelden-Etcherdingen
Germany

Bibliography

– Bouvier, Nicolas. L' Art populaire en Suisse. *Switzerland: Éditions Zoé, 1999.*

– Dawson, Tom and Judy. The Hochman Encyclopedia of American Playing Cards. *Stamford: United States Games Systems, 2000.*

– Depaulis, Thierry. Les Cartes de la Révolution, cartes à jouer et propagande (catalog compiled for an exhibition organized by the Musée Français de la Carte à Jouer, November 17, 1989–February 12, 1990). *France: Musée Français de la Carte à Jouer, 1989.*

– Depaulis, Thierry. 1984. Tarot, jeu et magie (catalog compiled for an exhibition at the Bibliothèque Nationale de France, October 17, 1984–January 6, 1985). *France: Bibliothèque Nationale, 1984.*

– Depaulis, Thierry. Les cartes à jouer au portrait de Paris avant 1701. *France: Le Vieux Papier–Musée Français de la Carte à Jouer, 1991.*

– Depaulis, Thierry. Cartiers parisiens du xixe siècle (revised edition). *France: Éditions Cymbalum Mundi, 1998.*

– Fournier, Felix Alfaro. Playing Cards: General History from Their Creation to the Present Day. *Stamford: United States Gaming Systems, 1982.*

– François, André. Histoire de la carte à jouer. *France: Éditions S.E.R.G. Freal, 1974.*

– Génardière, Claude de la. Sept Familles à abattre. *France: Éditions du Seuil, 2000.*

– Hargrave, Catherine Perry. A History of Playing Cards and a Bibliography of Cards and Gaming. *Mineola: Dover, 2000.*

– Seguin, Jean-Pierre. Les cartes à jouer au portrait de Paris de 1701 à 1778. *France: Le Vieux Papier–Musée Français de la Carte à Jouer, 1989.*

– Seguin, Jean-Pierre. Le Jeu de cartes. *France: Éditions Hermann, 1968.*

– Tilley, Roger. Playing Cards and Tarot. *Great Britain: Weidenfeld and Nicolson Ltd, 1967.*

– Vérame, Jean. Les Merveilleuses Cartes à jouer du xixe siècle. *France: Éditions Nathan, 1989.*

Web Resources:
www.heritageplayingcards.co.uk • www.wopc.co.uk • www.pagat.com
www.thehouseofcards.com • www.usplayingcard.com

... and not forgetting all the information I gleaned from the Musée Français de la Carte à Jouer database, edited by Agnes Barbier, curator, together with Gwenael Beuchet, whom I thank here for her kindness and enthusiasm.

In the same series

Collectible Corkscrews
Frédérique Crestin-Billet
ISBN: 2-0801-0551-5

Collectible Fountain Pens
Juan Manuel Clark
ISBN: 2-0801-0719-4

Collectible Lighters
Juan Manuel Clark
ISBN: 2-0801-1133-7

Collectible Miniature Cars
Dominique Pascal
ISBN: 2-0801-0718-6

Collectible Miniature
Perfume Bottles
Anne Breton
ISBN: 2-0801-0632-5

Collectible Pipes
Jean Rebeyrolles
ISBN: 2-0801-0884-0

Collectible Pocket Knives
Dominique Pascal
ISBN: 2-0801-0550-7

Collectible Snowdomes
Lélie Carnot
ISBN: 2-0801-0889-1

Collectible Wristwatches
René Pannier
ISBN: 2-0801-0621-X

Collectible
POCKET
KNIVES

Dominique Pascal

Flammarion

Collectible
CORKSCREWS

Frédérique Crestin-Billet

...arion

Collectible
WRISTWATCHES

René Pannier

Flammarion

Collectible
SNOWDOMES
Lélie Carnot

Flammarion

Collectible
MINIATURE
CARS
Dominique Pascal

DINKY TOYS 181
VOLKSWAGEN

Collectible
PIPES
Jean Rebeyrolles

Flammarion

Collectible
MINIATURE
PERFUME BOTTLES

Anne Breton

Flammarion

Collectible
FOUNTAIN
PENS

Juan Manuel Clark

Collectible
LIGHTERS

Juan Manuel Clarke

Flammarion

Photographic Credits

FA1134-02-XII
Dépôt légal: 12/2002